NEWTON PAGE

JOHN LAW OF LAURISTON

By

A. W. Wiston-Glynn, M. A.

NEWTON PAGE

NEWTON PAGE

John Law of Lauriston

By

A. W. Wiston-Glynn

Edited by Gavin Adams

First published as

'John Law of Lauriston
Financier and Statesman, Founder of the Bank of France,
Originator of the Mississippi Scheme, etc.'

First published by Newton Page 2010

1 3 5 7 9 10 8 6 4 2

ISBN 978-1-934619-03-2
Library of Congress Control Number: 2010921727

Printed in the United States of America
Set in Adobe Garamond Pro

CONTENTS

of coinage—Arraignment of tax collectors—Council of Finances consider Law's proposals unfavourably—Petition for permission to establish private bank granted—Constitution of the Bank—The Bank's success—The "Pitt" diamond and its purchase.

Law's notes become official tender—The Mississippi Scheme projected—Early explorers of Mississippi territory—Establishment of the West India Company—Its absorption of depreciated billets d'état—d'Argenson appointed Chancellor of France, and attempts extinction of National Debt—Law innocently involved in d'Argenson's fatal scheme—Saved from arrest by Regent—The brothers Paris and an anti-system.

Exaggerated accounts of resources of Louisiana—Law's judgment at fault—His ultimate aim—He creates an artificial rise in the value of Company shares.—His unsuccessful efforts to gain influence over Saint-Simon—Acquisition of Tobacco monopoly—Absorption of other companies—Reconstitution of West India Company—Parliamentary opposition overcome—*Mothers* and *Daughters*—Excited speculation in shares—Issue of notes to colonists—A pioneer's account of Louisiana.

Company acquires right of coinage—Issue of fresh stock and rise in price—Attempts made to discredit Law—Stair's account of the situation—Law defeats the anti-system—The concluding proposal of his schemes—The Company's capital and sources of revenue—Report of directors for 1719—Law's bank converted into a Royal bank against Law's wish—The Regent divests notes of the bank of their most valuable features—Provincial branches established—Restriction of gold and silver tender—Extravagance of successful speculators.

specie—Temporary success of remedy—Domiciliary visits resorted to for detection of hoarded specie—Bank and Company United—Discharge of National Debt—Use of the Rue Quincampoix prohibited as a stock market—The assassination of a stock-jobber by the Comte de Horn, and the latter's execution.

New measures prove ineffectual—New edict issued fixing price of shares and depreciating value of notes—Authorship of edict—People hostile to edict—Parliament refuses to register it, and a revocation is issued—Law deposed from office of Comptroller-General—d'Aguessau reinstated in his former office—New schemes for absorption of bank-notes—Widespread distress produced amongst community—Law's person in danger—Stock-jobbers establish themselves in the gardens of the Hotel de Soissons—Parliament exiled to Pontoise, and Bank closed for an indefinite period.

Starvation produced amongst poorer classes by issue of new edict—Law's expulsion from France demanded—Law resigns all his offices and leaves for Venice—Privileges of Company withdrawn—Commission appointed to value unliquidated securities—Law in vain applies for recovery of a portion of his wealth—His death at Venice—Attitude of French people towards Law—Circumstances to be considered in passing judgment.

CHAPTER I

Standard of criticism hitherto applied to John Law—Birth and ancestry—Education—Death of father—Early devotion to study of finance—Manner and appearance—Visits London—Duel with Beau Wilson—Tried for murder—Escapes to France—Meets Lady Catherine Knollys—Career of gambling on the Continent—Studies banking—Formulates new principles of finance—Returns to Scotland.

CHAPTER I

It has been the fate of most men who have left their name upon the pages of political history to have their conduct scrutinised with a degree of ethical fineness which happily is denied those whose records have not risen above the commonplace. Such a standard of criticism has been invariably applied in instances where origin of birth would hardly justify anticipations of pre-eminent greatness—and especially where the circumstances that have fostered its rise lie outside the beaten track, and possess the inviting charm of novelty. Reputation acquired in the steady, patient pursuit of a purpose is not more likely to reach the level of permanent fame, than one of which spasmodic progress forms the outstanding element. Where brilliance of meteoric splendour appears in any sphere of life, but chiefly in the region of national politics, a curiosity which otherwise would be escaped is aroused by reason of its suddenness, and attempts are made to discover unworthy motives behind each act. While these attempts can only have a problematic value in absence of any true disclosure of motive, judgment is not infrequently passed with an air of authority that seems to exclude refutation. Nor is it an uncommon occurrence for contemporary opinion, prejudiced and perhaps unjust, to distort the estimates of subsequent writers. Exemplification of this is in some degree to be found in the case of John Law of Lauriston, the founder of the Mississippi Scheme, whose chequered and questionable career before his elevation to a position of national importance in the government of France, furnished excellent material for a sinister interpretation of his intentions by his detractors.

By birth, Law belonged to a family which held a position of considerable social rank and influence in the Scottish capital. He was born at Edinburgh, on the 21st of April, 1671, and his father, William Law, described in the records of his time as a goldsmith carrying on business in the capital, followed a profession more nearly allied to that of banking as now understood. Some conflict appears to have existed as to his lineage, but on the authority of Walter Scott, Writer to the Signet, father of Sir Walter Scott, who acted for some time as agent for the family, it may be taken that Law was the grandson of James Law of Brunton, in Fife, by Margaret, daughter of Sir John Preston, Bart, of Prestonhall, and great-great-grandson of James Law, Archbishop of Glasgow from 1615 to 1632. The claim of his mother, Jane Campbell, to relationship with the ducal house of Argyll may have been somewhat remote, but is not at all improbable.

With a view no doubt to educating his son to a career which the fortunes of the family were sufficient to enable him to follow, and perhaps because he early perceived evidences of uncommon capacity, William Law embraced every opportunity which the educational facilities of the time afforded. In order to put him beyond the possible prejudicial influences of the city, he sent young Law at an early age to Eaglesham, where he was placed under the care of the Rev. James Hamilton, whose son subsequently married his eldest sister. There he received his early education in a school established by the Rev. Michael Rob, the first Presbyterian minister ordained after the liberty.

Unfortunately for the future of his promising son, William Law died in 1684, and to his mother's care, but probably less restraining influence, young Law was now entirely entrusted. In the year preceding his death, however, William Law had acquired territorial dignity by the purchase of the estates of Lauriston and Randleston, situated along the Firth of Forth a few miles west of Edinburgh, the right to which was taken in life-rent for himself and his wife, and in fee to John Law, their eldest son.

Law's mother, although no more than an ordinary degree of womanly grace and force of character can be attributed to her, possessed what was of equal, if not of greater, value at such a juncture as this, when the loss of the head of a family may mean so much a capacity to direct with prudence, tact, and business capacity the affairs of her estate. The family was large; of eleven children nine survived, and the burden imposed upon her resources by the education and maintenance of so many, without entailing at least outward change of appearance, is eloquent testimony to her cautious and careful management. Upon Law himself she bestowed the greatest concern, continuing his education upon the lines directed by his father, and in particular giving him every encouragement towards the study of mathematics, in which his youthful mind took the deepest delight. At an age when the majority of children have merely mastered the preliminary stages of a branch of knowledge presenting so many difficulties—and seldom indeed caring or willing to go beyond its threshold—Law was able to find the most genial occupation in solving the most complicated problems in geometry, and in comprehending the subtleties of algebraic formulae. At a time also when political economy as a science was undeveloped, and when the dominating principle of finance consisted of meeting daily exigencies by daily expedients, Law devoted a considerable portion of his time to inquiring into the basis of national and private credit, the laws governing the currency of money, the problems of taxation, and generally all the intricacies of economic phenomena that presented themselves to his observation. The theories which he formulated as scientific explanations of these phenomena indicate a philosophic grasp of mind, although they may now appear crude and untenable, and bear the marks of his proneness to hasty conclusion. They soon, however, procured for him distinction as an economist of novel ideas, and formed the foundation for the development of the various schemes by which he afterwards acquired a European reputation.

Added to his undoubted intellectual abilities, Law possessed an engaging manner, a generous disposition, and a handsome personal appearance. By his fastidiousness in dress, he gained a degree of notoriety amongst his fellows, and was known amongst the ladies of his acquaintance by the appellation of Beau Law, whilst the gentlemen of the city conferred upon him the nickname of Jessamy John.

When twenty-one years of age, Law, with the feeling of independence due to the competency with which he had been provided by his father, desired to find a wider field for the proper display of his various accomplishments, and accordingly found his way to London, whence he made frequent visits to Tunbridge Wells, Bath, and other popular places of pleasure of the day. There he mixed with the highest social and political circles, to which his talents obtained him ready access, but in a society where gambling, hard drinking, and general dissipation were marks of distinction, Law's popularity made serious inroads in a very short time upon his pecuniary position. An accumulation of debts necessitated a rearrangement of the fee of Lauriston in order to provide for their payment. This he conveyed to his mother in consideration of her advancing the requisite sum, and whatever other money he required for immediate and legitimate purposes. The burden thus imposed upon the estate, however, was not to be allowed to remain. By severe economy his mother was able within a comparatively short period to remove it, and to secure the estate free of encumbrance in entailed succession to her family.

An event, however, shortly occurred, which almost resulted in an ignominious termination to Law's career, but, as it happened, he succeeded in escaping its consequences although it necessitated his departure from the country. As an exponent of masculine fashions, he had a rival in one Edward Wilson, a younger son of a Leicestershire landlord. Their rivalry, as may be judged, did not conduce to friendly relations, and ill-concealed feelings of hatred existed between the two. This Wilson had been an ensign in Flanders, but having resigned his commission—from what cause it is not known, whether it was that his daintiness rebelled against the roughness of soldiery or that his courage was not equal to its dangers—he found his way to London, and there was a source of the greatest mystery to his friends and associates. Possessed of little or no patrimony, he yet maintained a magnificent establishment with an army of servants, and drove a coach and six. His lavish entertainments, and his social splendour, were the envy of the wealthiest. With unlimited credit, he nevertheless incurred no debts but were speedily paid, and on his death left no estate or evidence of the source of his abundant means.

With Wilson, Law had a serious difference, in which a Mrs. Lawrence, according to one account, and according to another Miss Elizabeth Villiers, afterwards Countess of Orkney, was concerned, and satisfaction could only be obtained by resorting to a duel. They met at midday on the 9th of April, in 1699, in Bloomsbury Square, and Wilson receiving a fatal wound, Law was arrested on a charge of having "of his malice aforethought and assault premeditated, made an assault upon Edward Wilson with a certain sword made of iron and steel of the value of five shillings, with which he inflicted one mortal wound of the breath of two inches, and of the depth of five inches, of which mortal wound the said Edward Wilson then and there instantly died." Law was tried on the 18th, and two following days of the same month at the Old Bailey, before the King's and Queen's Commissioners, but notwithstanding the most skilful defence, was found guilty of murder, and condemned to be hanged.

His popularity with persons of rank now stood him in good stead at this critical juncture. The acquaintanceships he had assiduously cultivated during his brief stay in London were not without their value, and enabled him to draw upon their influence to serviceable purpose. The King's mercy was invoked, and pardon was extended to the condemned man. His release, however, was not to bring him absolute freedom. An appeal was immediately made by Wilson's brother to the Court of King's Bench to have this apparently wrongful exercise of royal clemency cancelled. So general was the impression that justice had been flagrantly abused, that Law was again arrested and thrown into prison during the dependence of the appeal. Numerous technical objections were taken to the grounds of the charge, but all without success, and fortune seemed at last to have handed him over to the doom already pronounced against him. But expedients for escape had not been all exhausted. With the assistance of his friends he contrived, two days before his execution, to regain his liberty, and place his recapture beyond possibility. After overcoming his guard by the use of an opiate, and removing the irons with which he had been fettered by means of files surreptitiously conveyed to him, he climbed the high wall encircling the prison buildings, and, in the company of sympathetic associates, succeeded in reaching the Sussex coast, where a boat had been held in readiness to convey him over to France. The authorities made no serious effort to prevent his flight. Rather does it appear that, under the influence which formerly secured his pardon, they connived at his escape. Strength is given to this hypothesis by the misleading description of Law in the announcement offering a reward for the capture of the fugitive, which appeared in the *London Gazette* on the 7th of January, 1695, to the effect that "Captain John Lawe, a Scotchman, lately a prisoner in the King's Bench for murder, aged 26, a very tall, black, lean man, well shaped, above six foot high, large pock-holes in his face, big high nosed, speaks broad and loud, made his escape from the said prison. Whoever secures him, so as he may be delivered at the said prison, shall have fifty pounds paid immediately by the Marshall of the King's Bench."

Having arrived in safety upon French territory, Law made his way to that haven of refuge for all needy Scotsmen of birth and influence, the Court of St. Germains. Here he hoped to recover his lost position and fortunes by placing the services of his naturally great abilities at the disposal of a Court to whom they could not but be of some advantage if properly directed. His efforts to secure a place were unsuccessful, but it was probably at this time that he met the lady who was afterwards to be his wife, although for a time she lived with him as such while yet she was the wife of another. Lady Catherine Knollys, sister of the fourth Earl of Banbury, was the wife of a gentleman called Senor or Seignieur. Law's attractions were probably too captivating to be resisted, with the result that she "liked him so well as to pack up her alls, leave her husband, and run away with him to Italy."

The moral obliquity of the incident lends colour to the unsparing attacks of his enemies, and certainly cannot be extenuated even according to the loose standards of his day. The gravity of the offence he could not be ignorant of, notwithstanding his youth. His finer susceptibilities, however, had been impaired by the contagion of vice, which led him to embark upon risks, especially of gallantry, from mere impulsiveness, and regardless of consequence. What little credit can be extended to Law in connection with this affair, he derives from having remained faithful to her to the last, while the death of her husband, shortly after, relieved him of possible embarrassment during his subsequent visits and residence in Paris.

Unsuccessful in his appeal to the Court at St. Germains to secure official employment, he resumed his old career of gambling, and made the principal cities of the Continent the field of his operations for the next three or four years. His movements at this time are somewhat difficult to trace. No authentic record of his peregrinations has come down to us. It is tolerably clear, however, that he resided for short periods at Genoa, Rome, Venice and Amsterdam, and may also have visited Florence and Naples. Gambling in his case was no mere means of satisfying an uncontrollable passion. He did not conduct it promiscuously. He based his speculations upon a system which he had developed for his own guidance after the most careful study of the laws of chance. Although success did not invariably attend his play, the balance of probability was so frequently in his favour that he was not only able to maintain his position as a gentleman of worth, but to amass a considerable fortune in an incredibly short period of time. No doubt the cool, calculating Scotsman, apart from any merit his system of play may have possessed, was more likely to rise from the tables with success than those with whom he would choose to gamble. Not only would his confidence and boldness irritate and excite his opponents, but the reputation his skill had acquired for him would be in itself a disturbing element to their minds, and render them unequal to his superior play.

Notwithstanding his propensities in this direction, Law also devoted his abilities and his keen powers of observation to another and more creditable study. The subject of banking, the mysteries of credit, and all the intricacies of financial problems appealed to his strongly mathematical mind, and of the advantages afforded him, whilst on the Continent, for an intimate acquaintance with the various systems of his time he was not slow to avail himself, At this period there were several banking companies in Europe, and of these the banks of Venice, Genoa, and Amsterdam were the chief. The first two owe their origin to the financial difficulties of the Venetian and Genoese republics, and had been in existence since 1157 and 1407 respectively. The Bank of Amsterdam, on the other hand, was of more modern growth, having been established in 1609 in order to minimise the confusion continually arising from the unsteady value of the currency by placing the coinage upon a fixed and more permanent basis. Law, accordingly, utilised his stay in these three cities to gaining an insight into their methods of business. At Venice, we are told, he constantly went to the Rialto at change time, and no merchant upon commission was more punctual. He observed the course of exchange all the world over; the manner of discounting bills at the bank; the vast usefulness of paper credit; how gladly people parted with their money for paper, and how the profits accrued from this paper to the proprietors. At Amsterdam, where he was employed as secretary to the British Resident in Holland, "he made himself acquainted on the spot with the famous bank of that city; with its capital, its produce, its resources; with the demands individuals had upon it; with its variations, its interests; with the mode of lowering or raising its stock, in order to withdraw the capital, that it might be distributed and circulated; with the order that bank observed in its accounts and in its offices; and even with its expenditures and its form of administration."

The varied information which Law in this way acquired during his residence on the Continent, and especially in the great banking centres, he did not store as a mere mass of bare interesting facts. Whether the investigations he assiduously pursued were the outcome of a design to develop a new system of banking, or proceeded merely from the attraction of the subject, is matter of doubt. But it is clear that he abstracted certain principles of finance from the data he had gathered, and that these principles were heterodox according to the opinions of his contemporaries. Our judgment upon Law must be largely determined by our impression as to whether these principles were logically deduced explanations of the financial phenomena he observed, or whether they were the fanciful ideas of his own imagination for the justification of which he sifted his phenomena. It is extremely difficult to arrive at any definite conclusion. His own published writings give no guiding clue, and the records of his time confuse, rather than enlighten, by their contradictory and varied explanations of his schemes. It is probable that the principles upon which they were founded possessed an element of both possibilities. His observations on the one hand would seem to indicate to his mind some underlying law; and on the other hand his mind, impressed with the beauty and simplicity of some vast ambitious scheme of finance, would readily discover support in its favour from the deductions he had made. At no time did Law attempt to build up a system of financial philosophy, but he must be given due praise for laying down propositions bearing upon the subject of credit and of the use of paper money which have stood the test of time and received recognition from political economists of our own day. He must also be raised to a higher level than a mere financial schemer. His proposals were more than plausible. They had an element of practicability, in which he demonstrated his own belief by his readiness to put them to test under private direction before they were launched with sovereign authority and under public control. Convinced so thoroughly as he was with the soundness of his theories, and with the possibilities they opened up, if adopted, of infusing new life and new energy into the commercial world of his day, he regarded himself as a man with an important mission.

His own country seemed to offer a suitable field for his financial ability, and we find him back in Edinburgh in the closing year of the seventeenth century, the legislative independence of Scotland affording him all necessary safety against arrest for the murder of which he had been guilty five years previously.

CHAPTER II

Unsettled condition of Scottish politics in 1700—Financial
and commercial insecurity of country—Law's solution of
difficulties—Land Bank—Supported by Court party—Rejected
by Parliament—Again resorts to gambling—Returns to
Continent—Expelled from Holland—Visits Paris—Discusses
finance with the Duc d'Orléans—Expelled by Lieutenant
General of Police—Submits proposals to Louis XIV without
success—Again attempts to secure adoption of proposals
by France—Financial condition of France—Earl of Stair's
friendship with Law.

CHAPTER II

Scotland at the time of Law's return was in a very unsettled condition, politically and commercially. The projected union of the two kingdoms was beginning to emerge from the sphere of discussion into that of practical politics. The change was recognised as likely to be attended with results of the greatest consequence, but was not by any means enthusiastically supported by public opinion. What, however, was obviously impossible by means of conviction, was ultimately accomplished by methods of bribery, and the Act of Union stands as a striking instance of the great success of a policy universally condemned, but carried by dishonourable means in spite of the opposition of those who were chiefly concerned.

The minds of the people, however, in 1700 were more disturbed by the feeling of financial insecurity that was gradually asserting itself. The air had been for some years laden with all kinds of fanciful schemes advanced by men who had the public ear, and who had succeeded in calling up visions of easily won wealth in the imaginations of a nation at that time, as now, characterised by caution and business prudence to the degree of frugality. Banks, colonisation schemes, and all sorts of extravagant and even ridiculous proposals followed close upon one another in one continuous stream, but almost invariably bringing ruin in their train. The most notable, as it was the most disastrous of these, was the Darien Scheme launched by William Paterson, founder of the Bank of England. Patronised by all the nobility and people of money as well as by numerous public bodies, and possessing all the superficial elements of success, it produced a fever of financial excitement and a mad race for the acquisition of holdings in its capital. Its collapse caused widespread disaster, and was in reality a national calamity, entirely destroying that confidence essential to industrial and commercial stability.

Law found in the condition of his native country a congenial subject for treatment according to the economic theories he had developed during his stay on the Continent. In the beginning of 1701 he published his *Proposals and Reasons for Constituting a Council of Trade in Scotland*. In it he advocated changes of a very drastic and radical character, and while they were without question too advanced and impracticable for his day, at least for adoption in their entirety, they show that he was by no means a utopian theorist, but possessed the insight and foresight of a statesman. He advocated the establishment, under statutory authority, of a Council of Trade entrusted with the sole administration of the national revenue, bringing under that denomination the king's revenues, the ecclesiastical lands, charitable endowments, and certain other new impositions, such as a tax of one-fortieth on all grain grown in the country, one-twentieth of all sums sued for by litigants, and a legacy duty of one-fortieth. The Council of Trade would control the national treasury and would direct the national expenditure. The uses to which he suggested the moneys thus collected should be directed were all devised in the interests of promotion of trade. After allowing a sufficient sum for the Civil List, the Council were to discover proper means of employing the poor and preventing idleness; establish national granaries; improve the mines and develop the mineral wealth of the country;

restore the fisheries to their flourishing condition of the reign of James I; reduce the interest of money abolish monopolies; and encourage foreign trade, which was at a very low ebb. Notwithstanding the vigour with which Law advocated his proposals, and notwithstanding the brilliant hopes he held out by their adoption, they received little or no countenance from public opinion, and were regarded as wholly impracticable by Parliament.

During the five years that followed his first unsuccessful incursion into the domain of practical politics, Law was engrossed in the development of a new and more brilliant project. He gave it to the world in 1705 in a volume which bore the title, *Money and Trade Considered, with a Proposal for Supplying the Nation with Money.* It displayed a remarkable grasp of the theory of credit, and evidenced the inborn financial genius of its author. Although its proposals and the propositions upon which they were based can hardly bear judgment according to the standards of present-day political economy, it must be remembered that up to that time no attempt had been made in the formulation of the principles of that science. The difficulties he had to encounter were great, but the manner in which he surmounted them was not only a tribute to his clearness of mind, but showed a judicial capacity to a remarkable extent in marshalling masses of disjointed facts.

He proposed the establishment of a land bank, with power to issue to landlords notes secured upon their estates, and having a forced currency at their face value. The extent of each issue was to be determined in one of three ways: (i) As an ordinary heritable loan, not exceeding the maximum of two-thirds of the value of the property; (ii) As a loan up to the full value of the property, but with a fixed period of redemption; or (iii) As an irredeemable purchase for value. The adoption of his proposal would have had the effect, he submitted, of relieving the commercial tension due to the insufficiency of specie by supplying a medium of currency of a non-fluctuating value. Though forced, the notes would not in any way have been mere accommodation paper, but would always be for value or security received. Confidence would thus have been maintained, and the risk of panic amongst holders avoided.

Law had succeeded in interesting the Court party and a considerable number of influential politicians in favour of his suggested scheme. It appealed to them less upon its merits than upon its probable effect of reducing the estates of the kingdom to dependence upon the Government. The Duke of Argyll, supported by his sons the Marquis of Lorne and Lord Archibald Campbell, and by the Marquis of Tweeddale, submitted the proposal to the Scottish Parliament. An opposition, however, led by the Lord Chancellor, proved strong enough to reject it by a large majority, and passed a resolution "that the establishing of any kind of paper credit, so as to oblige it to pass, was an improper expedient for the nation." It is evident that the ground of the opposition, which was ostensibly the chimerical nature of the scheme, but really the fear that the Government of the country would be placed in the hands of the Court by its adoption, was not the concealed intention of Law in its formulation. The possibility of this consequence only emerged in the course of discussion, and in the knowledge of the composition of Parliament the opponents of the scheme were strongly justified in regarding the possible result as a certain probability. From Law's point of view, however, the scheme only attempted what is successfully followed by banking institutions of the present day, with the difference that the latter have a reserve of gold against their notes, whereas the former would have had the landed property of the country.

Law's hopes of being able to realise his ambitions in his native land were now at an end. He saw no prospect of attaining that position in the control of public affairs to which he aspired, and for which he considered himself eminently fitted. He was, accordingly, compelled to fall back upon his old gambling career, which had been practically suspended since his return to Scotland. To such advantage did he indulge his skill in this direction, that in the course of a few months he found himself an extremely wealthy man, amongst his gains being the estate of Sir Andrew Ramsay of a yearly value of £1200 Scots, and an annuity of £1455 Scots secured upon the estate of Pitreavie in Fife, purchased in 1711 by Sir Robert Blackwood from the Earl of Rosebery.

The negotiations for the union of the two kingdoms were now fast approaching a successful conclusion. Law felt his safety in a somewhat precarious condition, the death of Wilson still rendering him liable to arrest should he cross the border, and the union in all probability likely to remove the element of safety from his residence in Scotland. He petitioned the Crown for a pardon, but Wilson's brother, an influential banker of Lombard Street, protested against its being granted, thus leaving no excuse upon which a pardon might be extended, had the royal prerogative been inclined in his favour.

The Continent furnished the only safe asylum, and thither Law removed himself in 1707, or at the latest, early in 1708. He seems first to have taken up residence at the Hague, and then at Brussels, living in luxurious fashion, and impressing every one by his extravagance and apparently inexhaustible resources. With a keen eye for the weaknesses of a people, Law introduced the Dutch to the exciting possibilities of the lottery system. So far was he received into their good favour that not only was a state lottery established, but every town of any consequence had a smaller lottery of its own. The lottery was to be the great panacea for all financial embarrassments, national and municipal. Law, however, was not a disinterested participant in all these dazzling schemes. His suggestions, if worth adoption, were worth remuneration, but unfortunately he did not himself disclose the source of it, with results which necessitated his removal from the country. "Mr. Hornbeck, Great Pensionary of Holland, being also a nice calculator, finding out that Mr. Law had calculated these lotteries entirely to his own benefit, and to the prejudice of the people, having got about 200,000 guilders by them, Mr. Law was privately advised by the States to leave their dominions."

On his expulsion from Holland, Law abandoned himself to the life of a rover amongst the various continental cities, and to all the attractions they offered. For six years he exercised with profitable results his skill as a gambler, and quickly gained a notoriety throughout Europe as a player of remarkable and unvarying success in every game of chance. He seems first to have gone to Paris, which afforded a rich and extensive field for gambling operations, and his good fortune brought around him a cringing crowd of followers, hoping to attract to themselves some of the glamour that surrounded the person of their idol. In his train were to be found the flower of the French nobility. He spent his time in the houses of the aristocracy of the day, of whom he was at all times a favoured guest, not less by his skilful play than by his pleasant, affable manner, and brilliant conversation and wit. Faro was the game in which he most delighted, and at the houses of Poisson, Duclos, and at the Hotel de Gesvres, he held a sort of faro bank, and the entree to these houses was considered a matter of the greatest favour. In the fashionable crowd of excited gamesters Law was the only one who remained absolutely cool whatever the fortunes of the game. His operations were conducted upon a most extensive scale, and necessitated the employment of considerable sums of money. It was no uncommon circumstance for Law to carry with him 100,000 livres or more in gold. So cumbrous did this become, that he conceived and carried out the idea of utilising counters, which were valued at eighteen louis each, and proved more convenient than the coin they represented.

During this first visit of Law to Paris, which apparently lasted not more than a year, Law succeeded in gaining the good favour of the Duc de Chartres, afterwards, as Duc d'Orléans, Regent of France during the minority of Louis XV, and of Chamillard, the Comptroller-General. With these he had frequent conversations concerning the embarrassed condition of the French treasury, and discussed proposals for its improvement. He captivated them by the apparent soundness of his knowledge of finance, and by his brilliant theories for the establishment of the National Exchequer on a stable foundation. Every opportunity was embraced by Law for holding these discussions, and although they had no immediate effect beyond securing the adherence of two of the most powerful men in the Government, they laid the foundation of his future greatness. Unfortunately, however, for Law, the continuity of his acquaintance with the man with whom he desired most to cultivate friendship was rudely and unexpectedly suspended. D'Argenson, Lieutenant-General of Police, was suspicious of Law and his methods. His reports to the Government were unfavourable and framed with a view to Law's expulsion from Paris. This he ultimately succeeded in getting authority to do, and Law was immediately served with a notice to leave the capital within twenty-four hours on the ground "that he knew how to play too well at the games he had introduced."

For a considerable time Law remained away from Paris, visiting the principal cities of Italy, Hungary, and Germany, and in all leaving behind him the reputation of being one of the most remarkable men of his age. He became a frequent and well-known visitor at all the gambling resorts on the Continent. His progress from city to city resembled the progress of a royal court, and rumour preceded him to herald his coming. He was no common gambler. He was an accomplished man of the world, exquisitely courteous, and with interests that rose above the sordid pursuits from which he derived his pecuniary prosperity. His political instincts were always allowed free play, and by close observation he acquired the amplest knowledge of the industrial and economic conditions of the various countries he visited.

Law was now becoming anxious to secure an opportunity of putting into practice the schemes he had mentally constructed for the improvement of trade and commerce. The more he observed the prevailing unhealthiness of industry, and the more he satisfied himself as to the apparent causes of industrial depression, the more did he feel that his scheme was the only royal remedy. He accordingly returned to Paris shortly before the close of the reign of Louis XIV, purposing to gain the support of that monarch for the adoption of his system in France. Chamillard did not now occupy the office of Comptroller-General, but Law through the influence of the Abbé Thesul was received by Desmarets, his successor, who not only discussed in thorough detail the scheme laid before him by Law for the rehabilitation of the financial condition of the country, but became so enamoured of it that he decided upon submitting it to the King himself. Louis XIV, however, was not a man of large mental horizon. His decisions were often the outcome of the impulse of the moment. Frequently they were determined by religious bias, even where religious scruples were wholly foreign to the matter under consideration. Law's proposal seems to have been placed under the latter category by Louis XIV. Report has it that the bigoted monarch was more anxious to learn the faith to which the Scotsman belonged than to know the merits of his scheme, and that on being informed Law was not a Catholic, he brushed aside the matter and refused to accept his services.

Disappointed, but not discouraged, Law was more determined than ever to have his system put to practical test. If France did not accept salvation at his hands, he doubted not some other country would. He accordingly approached the King of Sardinia, one of the needy sovereigns of the day. Law's proposal to him was the establishment of a land bank, which he held out in glowing terms as the certain foundation of great national prosperity, but the wily monarch was not to be drawn, and with a touch of sarcasm recommended Law again to urge his scheme upon France. "If I know," he said, "the disposition of the people of that kingdom, I am sure they will relish your schemes; and, therefore, I would advise you to go thither."

The end of 1714 saw Law for the third time in Paris. Whether his return to France was due to the suggestion of the King of Sardinia, or to his having perceived a possibility of his system being yet adopted by France, whose crippled financial condition was becoming more serious as time went on, and demanded some drastic remedy to relieve the intolerable burden upon the Treasury, we cannot judge. He probably considered that, with bankruptcy hanging over the French nation like a grim spectre, necessity, if not conviction, would induce the acceptance of his theories. The nation's indebtedness had now outgrown its resources. Every conceivable device had been resorted to for the purpose of meeting the most pressing obligations. Provision for the future was regardlessly sacrificed to the needs of the moment, and ingenuity was devoted only to keeping the evil day afar off. Everyone feared the worst. No one was able to grapple with the difficulty in a broad, statesman-like fashion, and to carry out a bold policy of national economy. The treasury had to face the payment of exorbitant rates of interest upon loans, the full value of which had not been received. The coinage was debased to an extent altogether out of proportion to its face value. Lotteries were organised on an extensive scale as a means of appealing to the gambling instincts of the community, and as a method of applying indirect taxation without the hateful element of compulsion. *Billets d'état* were foisted upon unwilling creditors in almost unlimited amounts, and formed a paper currency that had difficulty in changing hands at even ten percent, upon its value of issue. To crown all, titles were sold as mere articles of commerce, sinecures created with high-sounding designations that roused the ridicule of the multitude, but helped to provide the king with money, and monopolies granted to the highest bidder. Yet all these devices failed their purpose, and the insatiable hunger of the treasury was still far from being appeased. Financial paralysis was creeping over the nation, and threatened the gravest consequences.

Here was such a field as Law alone could fully appreciate. Fortune at last seemed about to smile upon him. His star was about to assume a meteoric brilliance, and to mount towards its zenith with marvellous rapidity. Circumstances moulded themselves to his successful progress; and with rare capacity Law took full advantage of every opportunity. In order to remove as far as possible, social obstacles to his easy access to Court, he took up residence in a fine mansion, and lived as a man with unlimited means at his disposal. He entertained, in the extravagant way that marked his previous visits to Paris, all those whom he thought he could utilise for his own advancement; and the death of Mr. Segnior enabled him to marry the latter's widow, with whom he had hitherto been living, thus removing the taint of illicitness from his cohabitation with her, and legitimising his family.[1]

Law's objective was the good favour of the Duc d'Orléans. He recognised the importance of obtaining the support of the

1.Ed. Note. Although Lady Catherine Knollys became known as Lady Catherine Law, she and John Law never married.

man who promised to occupy the regency within a very short time, and who would thus possess sufficient power to impose upon the government any scheme towards which he was favourably inclined. With great prudence Law did not seem to be over-anxious in the prosecution of his aim, lest he might induce suspicion as to his disinterestedness. He, accordingly, devoted himself at first to the entertainment of the prince by bringing into play all his varied gifts, and by gratifying his tastes for gambling and pleasure as far as he was able. "His good address and skill at play, made him particularly taken notice of by the regent, who used to play with him at backgammon, a game the regent likes mightily, and Mr. Law plays very well at." By this process, Law succeeded in placing his intimacy with the Duc upon a solid foundation, and in securing his influence when the opportune moment arrived for its exercise.

Law's fame as a potential financier of national grasp was at this time exercising the minds of the British Government of the day. The Earl of Stair had been newly appointed Ambassador to the Court of France, and was so impressed with Law's ability that he recommended him to Lord Halifax and to Secretary Stanhope as a man who might be useful in suggesting some means of liquidating the debts of the British Treasury, which at that time were somewhat complicated and assuming enormous proportions. On February 12th, 1715, Stair wrote to Stanhope:

"...There is a countryman of mine named Law of whom you have no doubt often heard. He is a man of very good sense, and who has a head fit for calculations of all kinds to an extent beyond anybody...Could not such a man be useful in devising some plan for paying off the national debts? If you think so, it will be easy to make him come. He desires the power of being useful to his country. I wrote about him to Lord Halifax... The King of Sicily presses him extremely to go into Piedmont, to put their affairs upon the foot they have already spoken of. I have seen the king's letters to Law, which are very obliging and pressing. I would not venture to speak thus to you of this man had I not known him for a long time as a person of as good sense as I ever knew in my life, of very solid good sense, and very useful; and in the matters he takes himself up with, certainly the cleverest man that is."

Shortly before this date Stair had written to Halifax in similar terms, and received the following reply of date February 14th, 1715:

"I had the honour to know Mr. Law a little at the Hague, and have by me some papers of his sent to Lord Godolphin out of Scotland, by which I have a great esteem for his abilities, and am extreme fond of having his assistance in the Revenue. I have spoke to the King and some of his Ministers about him, but there appears some difficulty in his case, and in the way of having him brought over. If your Lordship can suggest anything to me that can ease this matter, I should be very glad to receive it."

The latter portion of this letter obviously refers to Law's conviction of murder by the English courts, which Law had failed to obtain pardon for. On April 30th, 1715, Stanhope replied to Stair in the following terms:

"Though I have not hitherto, in my returns to your Lordship's letters, taken notice of what you have writ to me once or twice about Mr. Law, yet I did not fail to lay it before the King. I am now to tell your Lordship that I find a disposition to comply with what your Lordship proposes, though at the same time it has met, and does meet, with opposition, and I believe it will be no hard matter for him to guess from whence it proceeds."

Lord Stair's admiration of Law was very considerable, and so intimate was their friendship that we find the first entry in Stair's journal upon his arrival as British Ambassador in Paris in

1715 to be: "Wednesday, January the 23rd, at night, arrived at Paris; saw nobody that night but Mr. Law." Lord Stair's strong recommendations of Law to the British Government were based upon his fixed belief that his services would be of incalculable value. Law, himself, however, was not by any means anxious that they should be accepted. He saw greater scope in France for his financial schemes, and therefore, while permitting these friendly negotiations to proceed, he was somewhat indifferent as to their result.

He did not abate, on the other hand, his assiduous cultivation of the Duc d'Orléans; nor did he fail to please Desmarets, who, as Comptroller-General was in such a position as likely to become a powerful support in carrying out his plans. His relations with the Comptroller-General were also strengthened by the representations made to him by the Regent to encourage Law as a man whose advice at that critical period might prove of the utmost value. By his diplomatic conduct Law succeeded in having his proposal for the establishment of a land bank brought under discussion by the Council of Ministers. The result, however, was again unfavourable, the ground of rejection of the scheme, according to Stair's journal, being that there was no foundation for such a bank in a country where everything depended on the King's pleasure.

CHAPTER III

CHAPTER III

Louis XIV died on the 1st of September 1715, and was succeeded by his great-grandson Louis XV, then a mere boy of five years old. The Duc d'Orléans was called to the Regency, and wielded the power of an absolute monarch. He brought to his office the singular gifts of a statesman, and man of affairs, modified by the vices and indifference of a debauchée. The Duc de Saint-Simon speaks of the "range of his mind, of the greatness of his genius, and of his views, of his singular penetration, of the sagacity and address of his policy, of the fertility of his expedients and of his resources, of the dexterity of his conduct under all changes of circumstances and events, of his clearness in considering objects and combining things; of his superiority over his ministers, and over those that various powers sent to him; of the exquisite discernment he displayed in investigating affairs; of his learned ability in immediately replying to everything when he wished." No doubt this high estimate is the eulogium of a courtier, and requires to be discounted to some extent, but, on the whole, with little modification it may be considered a fair representation of the abilities of the man who was about to place Law in practical command of the government of France.

One of the first, as it also was one of the most important and pressing, matters to which the Regent's attention was demanded, was the financial condition of the country. The adoption of drastic measures was imperative. The national debt amounted to 3500 millions of livres, and while the revenue produced 145 millions, the expenditure of the Government absorbed 142 millions, leaving 3 millions with which to liquidate interest upon the national debt, or one-tenth of a percent. A deficit of 150 to 200 millions was thus accumulating each year, and every resource which ingenuity could conceive having long ago been exhausted, the situation was daily becoming more difficult. The Regent, shortly after his accession, called a meeting of the Council for the purpose of devising a means of relieving the intolerable strain. National bankruptcy was suggested by a few of its members, notably the Duc de Saint-Simon. The Regent would give no ear to such a course, and waved the suggestion aside as alike dishonourable and disastrous to all possibility of good government. No one, however, seemed capable of offering any plan of permanent value. The schemes proposed were merely expedients promising temporary relief, and no other policy but one of despair being apparent at the moment, the Regent was eager for their immediate execution.

A commission or *visa* was appointed to investigate the nature of the national debt, and, by classifying the claims, to bring order out of chaos. By methods, in many instances more rigorous than just, the national debt was reduced by 1500 millions, and interest was made uniform at the rate of four percent. Of the 2000 millions at which the debt now stood, 1750 millions were funded, and the balance of 250 millions was converted into a general floating debt represented by *billets d'état*. A substantial reduction was thus made in the amount of interest payable by the Treasury; but, without an increase of permanent revenue, which, if it were to be accomplished by the imposition of fresh taxation, neither the Regent nor his Councillors would face, or without a reduction in expenditure to an extent which would have rendered the public service inefficient, the solution of the financial difficulty was as distant as ever. Recourse was accordingly had to two measures, which served the purpose of the moment. The first was the old expedient of debasing the coinage. With the ostensible object of having a new currency with the new king's effigy, the old coinage was recalled. The fresh issue, however, was depreciated in the process to the extent of about thirty percent, and the Government profited by the transaction sufficient to liquidate one year's interest of the National Debt. The second device for replenishing the Exchequer was the establishment of a Chamber of Justice, a kind of inquisition for the investigation of the conduct of the tax collectors. These men by their unscrupulous dealings had come to be regarded as the evil genii of the French peasantry. Like vampires, they had for years been sucking the very life-blood of the nation. No redress was open to their victims, and resistance only had the effect of increasing the burdens laid upon their shoulders. The institution of the Chamber of Justice was accordingly received with unbounded joy. Every tax-farmer was arraigned before this tribunal. The most searching investigation was made, not only into his own dealings, but also into the dealings of the hordes of satellites whom he employed to bleed his unfortunate victims. Where information was withheld, or even where it was suspected that the information given was tainted with inaccuracy, encouragement was given to informers by holding out promises of twenty percent of any fines that might be levied. Such a system, of course, was bound to bring evils in its train as great as those it was intended to remove. A reign of terror set in amongst the farmers general. No sympathy was extended to them by their judges. All confidence in their honesty had long ago been destroyed. They were already prejudged. No effort on their part could by any possibility ward off the weight of accusation against them. Prison accommodation was soon taxed beyond its capacity. Those who were fortunate enough to

escape this Jeddart justice by bribery, by payment of enormous
fines, or by quietly submitting to wholesale confiscation, left
the country as a measure of personal safety. The records of the
period teem with the decisions of the Chamber of Justice and
their consequences. Most of the cases reflect a degree of moral
obliquity on the part of the judges not less than on the part of
the accused. We are told of one instance where a contractor had
been taxed, in proportion to his wealth and guilt, at the sum
of twelve millions livres. A courtier, possessing considerable
influence with the Government, offered to procure a remission
of the fine for a bribe of one hundred thousand crowns. "You
are too late, my friend," replied the contractor, "I have already
made a bargain with your wife for fifty thousand." In the
course of a few weeks almost the whole of the fraternity had
run the gauntlet of the Chamber of Justice. They had been
stripped of their power, their influence and their possessions.
The country had been effectively cleared of their presence,
but to comparatively small advantage. The total fines and
confiscations amounted to one hundred and eighty million
livres, of which the Government received only one-half, and
its parasites the other. As a consequence, its career was brought
to a close, and with it the ingenious financial devices of the
Council of Ministers.

Law was an amused spectator of the puerile efforts of the
Regent and his advisers to restore financial stability to their
country. He regarded them no less with scorn, and probably
rejoiced in the futility of their efforts, in the hope that each
successive step they took would bring the realisation of his own
ambition within measurable distance. The position he occupied,
however, was one of difficulty, and demanded a display of
considerable tact and judgment. He had educated the Regent
up to the point of implicit confidence in his scheme, but there
still remained a dead weight of opposition in the Council, and

without the support of both the ground was very uncertain.

No time was lost by Law in an attempt to bring his proposals to a head. He repeatedly interviewed the Regent within the first few weeks after the death of Louis XIV, and submitted definite schemes for relieving the situation. He urged that by the adoption of a system of paper credit, not necessarily for supplanting, but for supplementing, the coinage in currency, not only would the trade of the country increase in volume, but the national debt would be effectively dealt with. He based his argument upon the principle that the quantity of money in circulation in a country determines its industrial activity. Recognising that money, whether it be specie or paper, is not itself the wealth of a country, but only the measure of its wealth, and that in whatever form it exists it must represent either the whole or part of that actual wealth, he conceived the idea of issuing the notes against the landed property of France, and the ordinary State revenues. He pointed out, as examples in support of his proposals, the immense benefits which had flowed from the adoption of a similar system by England, Holland, Venice, and Genoa. The Regent, convinced before by Law's arguments, was now determined to put them into operation. He convened the Council of Finances, and invited to its deliberations the principal bankers and merchants of Paris and of the provinces. The sederunt took place on the 24th of October, 1715, only eight weeks after the King's death, but the Regent had personally interviewed beforehand several of the members to secure their support for Law. To this assembly Law unfolded the general outline of his proposals. "He was listened to as long as he liked to talk. Some, who saw that the Regent was almost decided, acquiesced; but the majority opposed." The precise ground of opposition is nowhere recorded, but probably the fear, expressed at the former Council in July, had not been dissipated, that the system would lend itself to abuse at the hands of an absolute monarch, and might bring in its train greater evils than those it was intended to remedy. The letters patent of the 2nd of May, 1716, granting private banking privileges to Law, refers to the decision of this assembly, but being couched in the language of official ambiguity, gives no clue to the reasons which actuated the rejection of the scheme. "Mr. Law having some time since proposed a scheme for erecting a bank, which should consist of our own money, and be administered in our own name, and under our authority, the project was examined in our Council of Finances, when several bankers, merchants and deputies from our trading cities being convened and required to give their advice, they were unanimous in the opinion that nothing could be more advantageous to our kingdom, which, through its situation and fertility, added to the industry of its inhabitants, stood in need of nothing more than a solid credit for acquiring the most extensive and flourishing commerce. They thought, however, that this present conjunction was not favourable for the undertaking; and this reason, added to some particular clauses of the project, determined us to refuse it."

Law was thus foiled again, but weakness of purpose was far from being a feature of his character. Irrefragable determination steeled him against all rebuffs. He saw more than ever that France was his last and only opportunity. He saw that the plastic minds of most of the ministers were susceptible to the pressure of the Regent's influence if applied with sufficient strength. This was not difficult of operation. The Regent's influence was at Law's command, and he made unsparing use of it. With prudent calculation, however, of the future, should his plans fail in their object by some mishap, he modified his scheme to the extent of petitioning for permission to establish a private instead of a national bank. In order, too, that the members of the Council and those who would be called to the deliberations in connection with his proposal should have some more definite and complete knowledge of his theories than could be conveyed in conversation, or in course of an address at the Council table, Law translated his book *Money and Trade Considered*, published in Edinburgh in 1705, supplementing what he had written there by separate papers giving his matured ideas.

Early in 1716 every preparation had been made, and all contingencies provided against. The Regent called again the Assembly of the previous October. The scheme was solemnly discussed. Opposition dwindled to a mere shadow. The scheme was passed, and remitted to the Regency Council for final ratification. This last stage in the process is well described by the Duc de Saint-Simon, whose opposition not even the Regent could overcome:

"M. le Duc d'Orléans took the trouble to speak in private to each member of the council, and gently to make them understand that he wished the bank to meet with no opposition. He spoke his mind to me thoroughly; therefore a reply was necessary. I said to him that I did not hide my ignorance or my disgust for all finance matters; that nevertheless, what he had just explained to me appeared good in itself, that without any new tax, without expense, and without wronging or embarrassing anybody, money should double itself at once by means of the notes of this bank, and become transferable with the greatest facility. But along with this advantage I found two inconveniences, the first, how to govern the bank with sufficient foresight and wisdom, so as not to issue more notes than could be paid whenever presented: the second, that what is excellent in a republic, or in a monarchy where the finance is entirely popular, as in England, is of pernicious use in an absolute monarchy such as France, where the necessities of a war badly undertaken and ill sustained, the avidity of a first minister, favourite or mistress, the luxury, the wild expenses, the prodigality of a King, might soon exhaust a bank, and ruin all the holders of notes, that is to say overthrow the realm. M. le Duc d'Orle'ans agreed to this; but at the same time maintained that a King would have so much interest in never meddling or allowing minister, mistress, or favourite to meddle with the bank, that this capital inconvenience was never to be feared. Upon that we for a long time disputed without convincing each other, so that when, some few days afterwards, he proposed the bank to the regency council, I gave my opinion as I have just explained it, but with more force and at length: and my conclusion was to reject the bank, as a bait the most fatal, in an absolute country, while in a free country it would be a very good and very wise establishment.

Few dared to be of this opinion: the bank passed. M. le Duc d'Orléans cast upon me some little reproaches but gentle, for having spoken at such length. I based my excuses upon my belief that by duty, honour, and conscience, I ought to speak according to my persuasion, after having well thought over the matter, and explained myself sufficiently to make my opinion well understood, and the reason I had for forming it. Immediately after, he edict was registered without difficulty at the Parliament. This assembly sometimes knew how to please the Regent with good grace in order to turn the cold shoulder to him afterwards with more efficacy."

Letters patent were issued on the 2nd and 28th of May, 1716, incorporating the Bank, and three days after the latter date, these letters were registered in the parliamentary journals. The Bank was formed under the name of the General Bank of Law & Company, the principal partners being Law himself and his brother William. The capital was fixed at six million livres, a sum approximately equal to £300,000, divided into 1200 shares of 5000 livres each. The price of the shares allotted to subscribers was payable in four equal instalments of which only one required to be in cash, the balance being in *billets d'état.* The management of the Bank and its general policy was placed in the hands of the shareholders themselves, the extent of their voting interest being determined by the number of their individual shares, each five shares conferring one vote. A bi-yearly audit was to be made of the Bank's financial position, and shareholders were to be convened at least twice a year. The business of the Bank was similar in its nature to ordinary banking business of the present day, and wise provision was made against engaging in commercial undertakings. In short, the regulations were modelled upon the soundest principles of finance. The one great feature of the Bank, however, and a feature that displayed Law's remarkable foresight, because its establishment was only the first step in the development of his vast designs whose ultimate accomplishment depended upon present success, consisted in the character of the note issue. All notes were drawn at sight to bearer, and were promises to pay in coin of the weight and standard of the day of issue. Here rested the foundation of the Bank's phenomenal success. The coinage had in previous years been subject to sudden and arbitrary changes of relative value, and consequently its purchasing power was always of a speculative character. But, further, as the Government alone secured the profit upon depreciation of the coinage, each alteration brought with it dislocation of commercial transactions and indirectly affected the volume of trade of the country. Law's notes in a very short time established themselves in the confidence of all classes. Their value was permanent and unaffected by any fluctuations in the coinage. Credit business was rendered possible where before it had been folly. Industry in general experienced the stimulus of financial stability, and underwent remarkable expansion. The notes, and not the current coinage, became the medium of exchange, and soon acquired a value in excess of the specie they nominally represented. To these advantages Law was careful to add ease of immediate conversion. Although the capital payable in cash only amounted to £75,000, yet the large deposits, and the extensive floating business of the Bank, together with the high estimate in which the notes were held, combined to make the risk of inability to convert the notes a very remote contingency.

In view of all these substantial advantages, the success of Law's scheme came in a measure as a matter of course. Business of the most profitable nature flowed into the Bank. By enabling commercial men to trade upon their securities at a low rate of interest, not only did he usurp the functions of the usurer, functions which the bad policy of the Government had placed in his hands, but the ramifications of the Bank spread throughout the whole country, and made its beneficent influences felt in a striking degree, Law himself very shortly became the supreme protector of industrial prosperity. His statesman-like instincts led him to revive many branches of trade which had degenerated, and to induce the establishment of others for which he saw the resources of France were eminently suited. In order to facilitate the business of the Bank he opened in the principal centres branch establishments which acted both as feeders and as outlets for the central institution. No one was more surprised than the Regent himself at the extraordinary measure of success which had attended Law's scheme. Law accordingly occupied more than ever a high position in the Regent's estimation. He was regarded as the financial saviour of France, a heaven-sent legislator before whom the hereditary advisers of the Crown were small and paltry. Law was sufficiently astute to press the advantage he had gained, and judging from the conduct of the Duc d'Orléans at this time, he evidently had the latter under his control. Saint-Simon tells us of the forced interviews he was compelled by the Regent to grant to Law in order that he might be tutored into approval, if not appreciation, of the new state of affairs. The wily courtier was impervious, however, to the blandishments of his tutor. He only deferred to the wish of the Regent, and merely gave a courteous acquiescence to the arguments and statements that were showered upon him. The object of these interviews obviously was to capture the confidence of Saint-Simon who had been sufficiently courageous on previous occasions to thwart Law's designs in face of the Regent's wishes, and who might prove an awkward element in accomplishing the development of his plans for the future. There was, however, a subsidiary purpose, and Saint Simon was not slow to recognise it. "I soon knew," says Saint Simon, "that if Law had desired these regular visits at my house, it was not because he expected to make me a skilful financier, but because, like a man of sense—and he had a good deal—he wished to draw near a servitor of the Regent who had the best post in his confidence, and who long since had been in a position to speak to him of everything and of everybody with the greatest freedom and the most complete liberty, to try by this frequent intercourse to gain my friendship, inform himself by me of the intrinsic qualities of those of whom he only saw the outside, and by degrees to come to the Council; through me, to represent the annoyances he experienced, the people with whom he had to do, and, lastly to profit by my dislike to the Duc de Noailles, who, whilst embracing him every day, was dying of jealousy and vexation, and raised in his path, underhand, all the obstacles and embarrassments possible, and would have liked to stifle him. The Bank being in action and flourishing, I believed it my duty to sustain it. I lent myself, therefore, to the instructions Law proposed, and soon we spoke to each other with a confidence I never have had reason to repent."

Notwithstanding the pressure of work upon Law's shoulders at this period when the enormous amount of details consequent upon the establishment of the Bank required his unremitting attention, he yet found ample time for indulging in those trifling matters which bulk so largely in the estimation of a courtier, and, especially if they entail extravagant expenditure, often cloud his limited horizon to the exclusion of affairs of greater importance.

The Duc de Saint-Simon, with a fine eye and a keen judgment for the dainty trifles of this world, had set his mind upon the purchase for the King of a priceless diamond which had come into the market early in 1717. This gem, variously known as the "Pitt" or "Regent" diamond, possessed a rather questionable history. It had been discovered in 1701 in the Parteal mines of the Great Mogul by a slave who immediately decamped with his precious find to the coast. Here he negotiated a sale with an English captain, who sold it to the Governor of Fort St. George, an office held at that time by Thomas Pitt, grandfather of the first Earl of Chatham. A model of it was made and shown to Law, who had been approached with a view to using his influence with the Regent for its purchase. The price, however, was a stumbling-block, and Law at once requested the assistance of the Duc de Saint-Simon. The Duc, who was always superior to any trifling financial difficulty, thought "that it was not consistent with the greatness of a King of France to be repelled from the purchase of an inestimable jewel, unique of its kind in the world, by the mere consideration of price, and the greater the number of potentates who had not dared to think of it, the greater ought to be his care not to let it escape him." Saint-Simon's record of his interview with the Regent is an excellent example of the arguments the extravagant spendthrift makes use of to salve his conscience when any whim is to be satisfied. The Regent "feared blame for making so considerable a purchase, while the most pressing necessities could only be provided for with much trouble, and so many people were of necessity kept in distress. I praised this sentiment, but I said that he ought not to regard the greatest King of Europe as he would a private gentleman, who would be very reprehensible if he threw away 100,000 livres upon a fine diamond, while he owed many debts which he could not pay; that he must consider the honour of the crown, and not lose the occasion of obtaining a priceless diamond which would efface the lustre of all others in Europe! That it was a glory for his Regency which would last for ever; that, whatever might be the state of the finances, the saving obtained by a refusal of this jewel would not much relieve them, for it would be scarcely perceptible; in fact, I did not quit M. le Duc d'Orléans until he had promised that the diamond should be bought. M. le Duc d'Orléans was agreeably deceived by the applause that the public gave to an acquisition so beautiful and so unique...I much applauded myself for having induced the Regent to make so illustrious a purchase." Through Law the price was fixed at two millions, or, approximately, £150,000. So reduced, however, was the exchequer that payment was impossible at the time, and thus an additional debt was added to an already over-burdened Treasury. The purchase of the gewgaw was a simple matter, and Saint-Simon was eminently capable for this portion of the negotiations. The payment was more difficult, and was postponed to be dealt with by Law himself.

CHAPTER IV

Law's notes become official tender—The Mississippi Scheme projected—Early explorers of Mississippi territory—Establishment of the West India Company—Its absorption of depreciated billets d'état—d'Argenson appointed Chancellor of France, and attempts extinction of National Debt—Law innocently involved in d'Argenson's fatal scheme—Saved from arrest by Regent—The brothers Paris and an *anti-system*.

CHAPTER IV

Less than one year's operations were sufficient to disclose the superior value of Law's Bank as an institution of national importance. Its remarkable success was not attributable to factitious or ephemeral circumstances, but to the confidence inspired by the soundness of the methods upon which its business was conducted. Law's powerful grasp of financial principles, and his striking capacity for their practical application, were evidenced in the masterly manner that characterised his management at this period. If anything was wanting to its complete success, it was recognition by the Government of the Bank as the official channel for the national revenues to reach the Treasury. This came before the first year expired. On the 10th of April, 1717, the Council decreed that the tax collectors should treat Law's notes as legal tender at their full face value. The effect of this, of course, was to extend the demand for so stable a medium of currency to districts as yet outside the sphere of the Bank's operations. Law's position was now one of the first magnitude. So far-reaching was his influence that the industrial welfare of France was bound up to a large extent with his fortunes, and would have been seriously menaced by its withdrawal. The stimulus of his activity was felt throughout the whole country, and secured for him the greatest authority and respect.

Law now considered himself in a position to develop another stage at least of his great scheme for the commercial regeneration of France. Not only was the moment opportune, but the principles he had been advocating in theory had operated so well in practice that he entertained no doubt that certain success would follow his new enterprise. Credit, and especially that phase of credit represented in paper currency, was capable, in his opinion, of unlimited expansion so long, at least, as there was an apparent foundation of security. With an available cash capital of only £75,000 he had been able to float and to give stability of value to 60,000,000 livres, or approximately £4,500,000. Why, therefore, not centralise the whole wealth of France and establish upon it a huge currency of notes, by means of which industrial growth and prosperity would be fostered?

Dominated by this one purpose, he projected his famous Mississippi scheme during the summer of 1717, a scheme which was at once to raise him to the highest pinnacle of fame and to prove his undoing.

France at this time possessed the vast American territories which are watered by the Mississippi. In 1674, Jolliat, who had been sent by the Count de Fontenac to discover if possible a passage through the Bay of California into the South Sea, came upon the great river, but did not attempt to explore it. This was accomplished by La Salle, one of the greatest French explorers of the American continent. He went out two years after Jolliat, and after many adventures and hardships, succeeded in navigating the Mississippi to its mouth, where he set up the French flag on the 9th of April, 1682, claiming the whole of the vast territory he had traversed for his native country. On making known his success to Louis XIV, he was furnished by that monarch with three ships and a man-of-war for the purpose of establishing a French colony in the region he had annexed, in order to establish the right of France to the newly-acquired territory. Unfortunately, La Salle was unable to again locate the mouth of the Mississippi, and, after several months of vain wanderings in quest of his destination, he was murdered by some of his followers, who had been exasperated by his ineffectual efforts, and goaded into revolt by his harsh and domineering disposition. D'Iberville, a French Canadian, who took up the task of exploration in succession to La Salle, enjoyed, however, greater success, and erected a French fort at the mouth of the river in 1712.

As yet no actual development of resources had been seriously attempted, but the glowing account of the vast riches of Louisiana given by d'Iberville had the effect of inducing a wealthy merchant, by name Antoine Crozat, to acquire the monopoly of its trade and of exploiting its natural wealth. Louis XIV granted him this privilege for a period of sixteen years from 1712. Whether by bad management, by bad fortune, by reason of the vastness of the undertaking, or by a combination of all three circumstances, Crozat, soon found he had entered upon a task, the magnitude of which was altogether beyond his capacity. In 1717, accordingly, he endeavoured to get rid of the burden he had so easily assumed, but could not so easily throw off. He naturally turned to Law, the man who loomed so large in the world of speculation, the one man who seemed able to evolve success from failure. Law regarded with favour the advances made by him, and created no little astonishment by announcing his decision to take over the monopoly and privileges which hung like a mill-stone round Crozat's neck. He intimated his decision to the Regent, and explained the course he intended to pursue in the development of his new proposal. The Regent, who was of course controlled in all financial matters by Law, was readily willing to comply with his wishes and countenanced the vigorous prosecution of the scheme.

In August, 1717, by letters patent, a trading corporation under the name of the West India Company was established. To it was given a grant of the whole of Louisiana, and for a period of twenty-four years from the 1st of January, 1718, it was to possess the sole rights of trading with the colony, and the company was generally to regard the undertaking as a huge commercial enterprise, in the management of which they would not be trammelled by State interference. For these privileges no payment was made to the State, but no act was to be allowed which might prejudice the sovereignty of France in Louisiana, and the company was under an obligation to furnish at its own expense all necessary military and naval protection. The capital of the company was fixed at 100 million livres, divided into 200,000 shares of 500 livres each.

Although no price was payable to the State for the apparently valuable rights acquired by the company, the ingenuity of Law had devised an indirect consideration of great importance. We have already seen how the Bank had absorbed depreciated *billets d'état* at their face value to the extent of four and one-half millions. But a bolder stroke was now conceived by Law. It was no less than to make the whole of the share capital of his new company payable in the State notes, which were then standing at a discount of sixty-five percent. These *billets d'état* formed part of the converted stock of the previous year, and bore interest at the rate of four percent. The company scrip which was given in exchange for the *billets d'état* was charged with a fixed permanent interest at the same rate, and in addition a contingent interest dependent upon the profits of each year. The effect of this financial juggle, was on the one hand, to transfer a twentieth part of the national debt from the State to a private company, and, on the other hand, to reduce the number of the nation's creditors by several thousands. The advantage was primarily in favour of the State, and as will be seen later, was the first step towards the total extinction of the nation's paper then in currency, by a method which in reality was repudiation of liability, though at this stage it could not have been foreseen as such either by Law or by the Regent.

The influential position to which Law had now attained was naturally productive of great heartburning, not only amongst those whose power he had virtually usurped, but also amongst the army of tax-farmers whose opportunities he had seriously curtailed. D'Aguessau, the Chancellor of France, was particularly envious of Law, and had used all his influence with the Regent against the new regime. Law, however, was paramount in the Regent's favour, and secured the summary dismissal of the undesirable Chancellor. In January, 1718, d'Argenson, Lieutenant of Police, a weak and pliable creature, was installed in his place, and a pretext was also discovered for requiring the resignation of the Duke of Noailles, chief of the Council of Finance, in order to combine the two offices in the person of d'Argenson. These appointments practically left the Government in the hands of the Regent, Law, and the Abbé Dubois, the Minister for Foreign Affairs. The elevation of d'Argenson was a move on the part of Law to secure the adoption of all his suggestions without encountering the opposition he would have met at the hands of a strong and independent Minister. His duties were to be merely clerical, and his services were to be at all times at the command of Law. D'Argenson, however, was of a suspicious disposition. Accustomed to being his own master in his former office, and active, though somewhat officious, in the administration of its functions, he fretted under the domination of his imperious master. He had been accustomed to the flattery of the great, and had become imbued with a sense of his own importance. To assume a position of inactivity, and to be deprived of all authority, were conditions much too humiliating to the self important Chancellor, and he endeavoured to surround his new office with an air of fictitious responsibility. While Lieutenant of Police, he had been accustomed to give audiences at all times of the night and day, and this furnished him with an idea as to the possibility of impressing the people with the false notion that he was more than ever immersed in public business. He made appointments at the most inconvenient hours, mostly after midnight or in the early morning, and those who were favoured with admittance carried away an exaggerated idea of the tremendous load of responsibility upon the shoulders of the new Chancellor, from a prearranged theatrical display of work in which he might be seen dictating to innumerable secretaries in the midst of a veritable ocean of papers and documents requiring attention. So far, indeed, did he carry this ludicrous performance, that he is said to have driven through the streets in the evenings with a lighted carriage in order to maintain the appearance of requiring to employ every moment of the day for overtaking the stupendous volume of work.

Behind all this mummery, however, there was a determination in the mind of d'Argenson to counteract the influence of Law, if not to supersede him altogether. With this object in view he conceived a bold plan for outbidding Law in his financial proposals. This was no less than the extinction of the floating national debt, and the means for its accomplishment was depreciation of the coinage. Law had provided for the absorption of 100 million livres in his Western Company, so that d'Argenson had set himself the task of taking up the balance of the State notes, amounting to 150 millions. His proposal was not only of the crudest, but it displayed an utter disregard for the industrial interests of France, and even he could not fail to have been impressed with the highly injurious effects upon trade of arbitrarily tampering with the currency. He secured, however, the adoption of his proposal, and on the

10th of May, 1718, a decree was issued debasing the coinage to the extent of fifty percent, upon the depreciation which took place in December, 1715. The silver marc was now raised from forty to sixty livres, and the crown piece of three livres ten sous, which weighed one ounce in 1715, now weighed less than half an ounce. In anticipation of his scheme, d'Argenson had purchased very cheaply a large quantity of silver for coinage purposes, and the Mint now issued sixty livres, weighing eight ounces, in exchange for forty-eight livres of the old coinage and twelve livres in *billets d'états*. In order, therefore, to absorb all the floating paper, d'Argenson required to issue 750,000,000 livres, upon which the State realised a profit of 250,000,000, so that after the cancellation of the notes there would therefore have remained a balance of 100,000,000. This high-handed proceeding created a deep feeling of resentment throughout the community, and Parliament, deferring to the wishes of the traders and of those who were affected by the change, issued on the 15th of June a decree practically annulling the whole of the new coinage. The Regent, whose authority was thus threatened, was in despair. He endeavoured to stem the tide of opposition by ordering the destruction of all copies of the decree, and forbidding its publication. Not to be outdone, however, the Parliament employed the services of men who were willing to expose themselves to the risk of being shot down by the soldiery whilst engaged in placarding the decree all the city of Paris. From Paris the opposition spread throughout the whole of France, and became almost revolutionary in its intensity.

Law's position had now unexpectedly become precarious. The outcry was directed towards him no less than the Regent, and d'Argenson, the real initiator of the fatal policy, was unconnected in the public mind with the agitation. Parliament, in the exuberance of its temporary success, resolved upon further measures. It instructed the collectors to refuse payment of; taxes in banknotes; it prohibited all foreigners from any share in the management of the national finances; and it withdrew the privileges of the bank in so far as these related to the administration of the Treasury. The climax was reached when Law was charged with the instigation of all the disastrous effects of d'Argenson's policy, and was under immediate danger of being arrested and forthwith hanged at the gates of the Palais de Justice.

It was now imperative that something should be done by the Regent. He felt that not only was he bound to save his favourite, but that, if Parliament were allowed without check to pursue its will, he also would lose his authority and mastery over the realm. Accordingly, a consultation was held on the 19th of August at the house of the Duc de Saint-Simon. "In this conference at my house the firmness of Law, hitherto so great, was shaken, so that tears escaped him. Arguments did not satisfy us at first, because the question could only be settled by force, and we could not rely upon that of the Regent. The safe conduct with which Law was supplied would not have stopped the Parliament an instant. On every side we were embarrassed. Law, more dead than alive, knew not what to say, much less what to do. His safety appeared to us the most pressing matter to ensure. If he had been taken, it would have been all over with him before the ordinary machinery of negotiation (delayed, as it was likely to be, by the weakness of the Regent) could have been set in motion; certainly, before there would have been leisure to think of better, or to send a regiment of Guards to force open the Palais de Justice; a critical remedy at all times, and grievous to the last degree, even when it succeeds; frightful, if instead of Law, only his suspended corpse had been found!"

Law, knowing the intensity of feeling with which Parliament was moved, and the certainty of their threat being carried out should they succeed in arresting him, was greatly concerned for his personal safety. A secure and ready asylum was at hand. The Regent placed at his disposal a chamber in the Palais Royal, an astute move on the part of those who suggested it, not only because it removed the possibility of Law's arrest, but because it would have the affect of strengthening the Regent's determination to undermine the authority of that insubordinate assembly. The suggestion emanated from the Ducs de Saint-Simon, and de la Force, and Fagon, one of the counsellors of state, all three virulent opponents of Parliamentary institutions. The presence of Law in the royal palace and the inadvisability of surrendering him to the tender mercies of the irate House were both strong incentives to the Regent to act at once with decision so as to secure the freedom of the powerful financier. A Bed of Justice was agreed upon by the Regent and his advisers as the only possible means of annulling the decrees of the 15th of June. The difficulties, however, in the way of its being held were great and required the utmost tact and secrecy. The Duc de Maine, suspected as the prime instigator of the parliamentary resolutions, and the Maréchal de Villeroy, a servile supporter of all the former's proposals, were regarded as possible successful opponents of a session of a Bed of Justice. Both were guardians of the young king, and as his presence was necessary to setting the seal of authority to the results of the deliberations of this body, the Regent feared they would place obstacles in the way. But the Duc de Saint-Simon was equal to the emergency, and, in his own voluble and consequential way, has recorded with much detail the measures he adopted for carrying out the proposal. He assumed responsibility for all the arrangements, and with gossipy fullness tells how he prepared for holding the Bed of Justice at the Tuileries, keeping it a profound secret until the very morning it was to be convened, and how the summons to attend was only to be issued a few hours before. The precautions although somewhat elaborate were all required. The step was highly critical for the Regent. It involved not only the recognition of his authority as Regent, but, in the event of its being unsuccessful, his deprivation of the Regency itself. In short, it could only be justified by a successful conclusion, a result which was ultimately attained, although by means of a high-handed and arbitrary nature. Throughout the whole of the proceedings, the Regent displayed a firmness and resolution which can only be attributed to the desperation of his position. They were sufficient, however, to the end he had in view, although by no means features characteristic of his general conduct. The Parliament was over-awed; the decree was abrogated; and Law once more regained his freedom. Thus was Law the innocent instrument of the degradation of the French Parliament, and the establishment of a despotism oriental in its thoroughness and far-reaching in its effects.

Law's escape from the violent intentions of the angry Parliament was however but a prelude to other difficulties and opposition. D'Argenson, smarting under the feelings of jealously engendered by the subordinate position he was compelled to play to a foreigner, and actuated by an exaggerated conceit of his abilities, conceived the notion of meeting Law on his own ground and damaging the importance of the latter by the adoption of a scheme which might supersede Law's by its brilliance and attract to himself the admiration of the financial world. Depreciated securities issued by the various government departments were afloat to incredible amounts. Their value was purely speculative, and any tendency to fluctuation was usually downward, so that unfortunate holders were always uncertain of the extent to which they might be calculated as realisable assets. Here was the groundwork of a scheme for the display of financial genius which might eclipse the schemes of Law by converting them at face value into securities of a more substantial and liquid character. The idea of conversion was of course merely an adaptation of Law's methods, but d'Argenson was bent on something less speculative, and so far as prospects were concerned, less remote, if not less illusory, than the Mississippi Scheme. He found ready instruments for his purpose in the four brothers Paris, great government contractors, men of considerable wealth, but most unscrupulous in the manner of their dealings. Not only were they envious of Law, but they feared a restriction of their own field of operations should his influence be left unchecked. With them therefore d'Argenson conspired in the initiation of a bold *anti-system*.

Their scheme was the formation of a company to take over a large proportion of the national revenues, and in payment of the shares, of which there were 100,000, of 1000 francs each, to take the depreciated securities of the public service at their full value. This company was to guarantee a revenue of 48 millions per annum, derivable from the sources of taxation allotted to them, and the treasury were to hold in security of their carrying out their obligation the 100 millions of depreciated securities which the company would absorb. The company would of course proceed in the manner usual to all farmers of the public revenue, and exact from the public taxation exorbitantly in excess of what was payable to the treasury. D'Argenson and the brothers knowing that the holders of the depreciated securities were thoroughly acquainted with the profitable nature of the business in which the company was to engage would only be too ready to convert their securities into the company's shares. The brothers Paris had a reputation for want of any quality of mercy in the levy of taxation, and the shareholders would require no assurances as to the probable returns upon their investments or as to the probable permanence of these returns. Alluring advertisements in praise of the company's sources of income were quite unnecessary as in the case of the Mississippi Scheme projected by Law. These unfortunately were patent to every one, but fortunately for those who would have been the victims of such a scheme, and fortunately also for the country at large, already suffering sufficiently from the insatiable rapacity of the tax-gatherers, the formation of the company did not commend itself to the Regent and his advisers, so once more Law was delivered from the jealousies of his rivals.

CHAPTER V

Exaggerated accounts of resources of Louisiana—Law's judgment at fault—His ultimate aim—He creates an artificial rise in the value of Company shares.—His unsuccessful efforts to gain influence over Saint-Simon—Acquisition of Tobacco monopoly—Absorption of other companies—Reconstitution of West India Company—Parliamentary opposition overcome—*Mothers* and *Daughters*—Excited speculation in shares—Issue of notes to colonists—A pioneer's account of Louisiana.

CHAPTER V

Law was now free to direct his thoughts to the business of the bank and the development of his original ideas with reference to the West India Company. Although the latter had been established in August 1717, nothing had yet been accomplished in the direction of actual business. The capital had been issued to an over-eager public, but unless a revenue were forthcoming the consequences would be grave for its originators. It was not sufficient that the flourish of trumpets with which he heralded the boundless possibilities of wealth of the vast and unknown territories of the Mississippi should die away with its last faint echoes. He must at once give evidence that the promises would bear fruit. The situation was difficult, but his ingenuity was equal to the task imposed upon him.

Since the establishment of the company, France had been deluged with books, pamphlets, engravings, and all kinds of advertisements and prospectuses descriptive of the extent and wealth of Louisiana. Exaggerated accounts were published of its riches, of its mineral resources, and of its people. One picture would exhibit mountains declared to be "full of gold, silver, copper, lead, and quicksilver. As these metals are very common, and the savages know nothing of their value, they exchange lumps of gold and silver for European manufactures, such as knives, cooking utensils, spindles, a small looking-glass, or even a little brandy." Another, designed to invest the natives with a highly religious disposition, would show them performing humble obeisance to the priests, and have accompanying letterpress to the effect that "the idolatrous Indians earnestly pray that they may receive baptism. Great care is taken of the education of their children."

Glittering accounts such as these appealed to the speculative instincts of everyone. All sorts and conditions of people sold their lands and purchased shares; ships were bought to carry intending emigrants; and transportation was substituted for all other penalties for criminals in order that a supply of manual labour might be furnished in opening up the newly acquired territories. Louisiana however was to prove a bitter disappointment to those who expected to find a country where hardships and difficulties were absent, where without trouble or labour fortunes were to be amassed in the shortest time, and where without stint the pleasures and luxuries of home could be enjoyed to the fullest.

The brilliant pictures that were drawn of the capacities of Louisiana were undoubtedly largely exaggerated so far as its condition was at the time. With the knowledge of subsequent years they were however substantially accurate, but the development of these capacities required the expenditure of vast sums of capital and the lapse of many years of hard and continuous labour of an imported population. The concessions made to the company on its incorporation were of enormous ultimate value, and under different conditions, conditions which would have imported fewer elements of speculation and introduced more administrative patience and moderation, might have proved a national asset of great importance instead of a disastrous enterprise the magnitude of which had the effect of paralysing for several generations the commercial and industrial stability of France. The concessions were co-extensive with virtual sovereignty over the vast territories included in the grant, and unlimited freedom of administration was conferred.

While it is evident that Law anticipated that Louisiana would in reality be a possession which would yield to his company a large annual revenue and prove an exceedingly profitable investment to its shareholders, it is equally evident that he recognised that this result could not be accomplished at once. He was probably mistaken as to the length of time that would be required, and, if so, he was only guilty of a fault of judgment attributable to the inadequacy of contemporary knowledge of these far distant lands as well as to the fact that experience of developing companies, such as the Western Company, was then in its extreme infancy. Until operations could proceed on a sufficiently extensive scale, the only immediate income derivable by the company consisted of the annuities payable by the Treasury, the amount of which was equivalent to interest at the rate of four percent upon the 100 million livres of State notes absorbed at the time of incorporation. From the fact that the first year's annuities of four million livres were to be devoted to the general purposes of the company, and that the succeeding years' annuities were to be placed to the dividend fund, it would seem that Law was under the impression that he could sufficiently develop the company's territories within a year to admit of further drafts upon the treasury payments being unnecessary.

On the other hand, the Western Company was but one element in the ultimate scheme which Law was ambitious to attain. His aim was to embrace in one vast undertaking not only the whole foreign trade of France, but also the large revenue departments of the government, such as the mint, and the collection of the national taxation. To these would be added the Bank, the success of which, in its present form, was now assured and had inspired the confidence of French people and foreigners alike. With these under one control, and all working together with one definite purpose, national prosperity might be placed upon a sound practical basis, trade in general be fostered and guided along lines of greatest development, and the circulation of money be more ample by the issue of notes to the extent of the real or approximate value of the incorporated assets.

During the early months of 1718, accordingly, he was engaged in laying plans for the acquisition of several monopolies and companies then in existence, but, by reason of indifferent management, not productive to their fullest capacity. In the meantime, however, the public required consideration at his hands. The shares of the Western Company were at a discount of fifty percent, and he foresaw the necessity before proceeding further of adopting measures to create a rise in their value to par at least, and if possible to a premium. His proposals would demand further appeals to investors, and their decision would inevitably be determined by the value in the open market of the stock he had already launched. The method he pursued to bring about this object was as ingenious as it was original. He offered to buy at six months' date in practically unlimited quantities shares of the Western Company at the minimum price of par and in many cases at a price in excess of par to the extent of twenty, thirty, and even forty percent. This proceeding naturally roused intense excitement, coming as it did from the prime mover in all the great financial operations which had so recently been agitating the community and been promising so great results. The consequence was as Law had hoped. The value of the shares was revived, the public were eager to join in the speculative fever that was produced, and Law not only employed their eagerness to his own advantage but succeeded in spreading and strengthening his already marvellous influence.

While Law was publicly carrying through transactions in such a manner as to rouse enthusiasm and inspire confidence in his projects, he was also at the same time engaged in securing by every possible means the good offices of those in high places without whose favourable support his plans would not likely reach maturity. The Duc de Saint-Simon reveals the nature of the efforts by which Law endeavoured to engage the good opinion of himself and others. "Law," he says, "often pressed me to receive some shares for nothing, offering to manage them without any trouble to me, so that I must gain to the amount of several millions. So many people had already gained enormously by their own exertions that it was not doubtful Law could gain for me even more rapidly. But I never would lend myself to it. Law addressed himself to Madame de Saint-Simon, whom he found as inflexible. He would have much preferred to enrich me than many others, so as to attach me to him by interest, intimate as he saw me with the Regent. He spoke to M. le Duc d'Orléans, even so as to vanquish me by his authority. The Regent attacked me more than once, but I always eluded him. At last, one day when we were together by appointment at Saint Cloud, seated upon the balustrade of the orangery, which covers the descent into the wood of the goulottes, the Regent spoke again to me of the Mississippi, and pressed me to receive some shares from Law.

The more I resisted the more he pressed me and argued. At last he grew angry, and said that I was too conceited, thus to refuse what the king wished to give me (for everything was done in the king's name), while so many of my equals in rank and dignity were running after these shares. I replied that such conduct would be that of a fool, the conduct of impertinence, rather than of conceit; that it was not mine, and that since he pressed me so much I would tell him my reasons. They were, that since the fable of Midas, I had nowhere read, still less seen,

that anybody had the faculty of converting into gold all he
touched; that I did not believe this virtue was given to Law, but
thought that all his knowledge was a learned trick. A new and
skilful juggle, which put the wealth of Peter into the pockets of
Paul, and which enriched one at the expense of the other; that
sooner or later the game would be played out, that an infinity
of people would be ruined finally, that I abhorred to gain at the
expense of others, and would in no way mix myself up with the
Mississippi Scheme.

M. le Duc d'Orléans knew only too well how to reply to me,
always returning to his idea that I was refusing the bounties of
the king. I said that I was so removed from such madness that I
would make a proposition to him, of which assuredly I should
never have spoken but for his accusation.

I related to him the expense to which my father had been
put in defending Blaye against the party of M. le Prince in years
gone by; how he had paid the garrison, furnished provisions,
cast cannon, stocked the place, during a blockade of eighteen
months, and kept up, at his own expense, within the town,
five hundred gentlemen whom he had collected together; how
he had been almost ruined by the undertaking, and had never
received a sou, except in warrants to the amount of five hundred
thousand livres, of which not one had ever been paid, and that
he had been compelled to pay yearly the interest of the debts
he had contracted, debts that still hung like a millstone upon
me. My proposition was—that M. le Duc d'Orléans should
indemnify me for this loss, I giving up the warrants, to be burnt
before him.

This he at once agreed to. He spoke of it the very next day to
Law; my warrants were burnt by degrees in the cabinet of M.
le Duc d'Orléans, and it was by this means I was paid for what
I had done at La Ferté. M. le Duc d'Orléans also distributed a
large number of the Company's shares to the general officers

and others employed in the war against Spain."

Law was by these means assured of the certainty of his coming proposals meeting with public approval, and the only step now remaining was to mature as speedily as circumstances would permit the arrangements he had been busily negotiating with the Regent and his advisers on the one hand and with the companies and the lessees of the various monopolies on the other.

The Tobacco monopoly was the first of the privileges to be acquired by the company. Although by no means an extensive trade, it was an important and lucrative one. The transfer was effected on the 4th of September, 1718, under burden of an annual charge of 4,000,000 livres payable to the king. Shortly after, arrangements were completed for the absorption of the Guinea Company, whose business was largely composed of slave dealing on the West Coast of Africa. This was finally carried through on the 15th of December of the same year. Then came the fusion of the French East India Company, established in 1664 by Colbert, and also a dormant monopoly issued in 1713 conferring the sole privilege of carrying on trade with China.

The Company was now assuming bulky proportions, and a re-arrangement of its capital was necessitated by the requirements of its wide and varied interests, and by the prospect of still further acquisitions under negotiation. Accordingly in May, 1719, a decree was published which conferred upon the Company the new and more pretentious title of the Company of the Indies; permission was given to increase the capital; and to the rights already possessed was added the monopoly of trade "from Guinea to the Japanese Archipelago, of colonising especially the Cape of Good Hope, the East Coast of Africa, that which is washed by the Red Sea, all the known islands on the Pacific, Persia, the Mougal Empire, the Kingdom of Siam, China, Japan, and South America." The increase of capital was fixed at 27,500,000 livres divided into 50,000 shares of 550 livres each, payable in monthly installments of 27 and one-half livres per share.

The magnitude of these transactions was now so great and unprecedented as to blind the public entirely to all other considerations, and enthusiasm for the foreigner was more than ever highly pitched. A mad scramble soon ensued for possession of shares which would produce so handsome returns as those promised by the great financier. Dividends of 200 percent were indicated as certain to accrue from the company's operations, and it is said that no fewer than 300,000 applications for shares were received from eager crowds of speculators. An unfortunate hitch, however, postponed the allotment to successful applicants. Parliament was still unwilling to follow Law into all his schemes. They were always ready to place obstacles in his path. Accordingly the decree authorising the issue of additional capital was refused endorsement, and six weeks elapsed before the difficulty could be removed. This untoward incident, however, by no means dampened the ardour of Law or of the general public. The previously issued shares of the Company which Law had been himself under necessity of converting from a discount to a premium were now in so great demand that they rose without his interference in the market. Artificial gave way to natural inflation of value through keen competition from without, and Law with that capacity for using every advantage with quick and ready skill turned the public feeling to immediate account. On the 20th of June he placed an absolute condition upon the acquisition of the newly authorised shares. With the ostensible object of laying down a standard for distribution of the new shares amongst applicants, but really of maintaining and if possible of increasing the price of the old shares, he expressed his intention of allotting the new shares in the proportion of one to four of the old shares held by the applicant. The purchase of the requisite amount of the original issue was a necessary preliminary to a favourable consideration of a further subscription. A great demand for original shares at once followed the issue of this decree, and accordingly the prices rose to double their face value within a comparatively few days. These shares were popularly known as the *Mothers* and the shares of the new issue as the *Daughters*. The excitement and competition was intense. The whole business of Paris seemed to be concentrated on the purchase and sale of Indian stock. From the highest down through every grade of the community to the lowest, every one talked and thought of nothing else. Visions of untold wealth were conjured up by rash participants in the race of reckless speculation, and the good fortune of many adventurers only served to stimulate those who as yet lagged far behind.

Forbonnais describes the effect of the decree. "When no more daughters were to be found, the western shares were sought for at any price. They were bought for ready money, or on credit with a premium on the price agreed on. Some sold so as to make sure of a large profit, and then seeing that the shares still went up, bought again. In such a state of fermentation, the quickness of the transactions did not admit of the employment of coin; the note was preferred to it; and so that the public might not want that, they did not put too high a price on it."

On the other hand, the absolute confidence which the Regent placed in the Mississippi Company, and his strong intention to render every assistance to the new colonists in the development of its resources, are seen in his consistent attitude of approval of all Law's proposals at this period. One of the difficulties with which the colonists had to contend was the absence, or at least scarcity, of a medium of exchange. Barter was much too cumbrous and inconvenient a method of exchange, and operated as a serious check upon freedom of commerce. Law's

solution was the issue of banknotes. The Royal Charter granted
at this time made provision for this, and the grounds upon
which the Regent, in name of the King, authorised the issue,
although probably inspired by Law himself, show also the steps
the company were taking for the exploitation of its territories.
"The King having by his Letters Patents of the month of August,
1717, established a Trading company, under the name of the
West India Company; and by his edict of May last, remitted to
the said Company the trade to the East Indies and China; His
Majesty sees with great satisfaction that that Company takes
the best measures for securing the success of its establishment;
that they send a great number of inhabitants to the country
Louisiana, which was granted them; that many private persons
make settlements in that colony, and send thither husbandmen,
tillers, and other handicraftsmen, to manure and improve
the land, sow corn, plant tobacco, breed silk-worms, and do
whatever is necessary to improve the country. Furthermore His
Majesty being informed that the said Indian Company is at great
charge for transporting the said inhabitants, and furnishing the
colony with meal and other necessaries, until the land affords
a sufficient quantity of provisions for their subsistence; that the
company sends thither all sorts of goods and merchandise, to
render the life of the inhabitants more comfortable; and that for
preventing of abuses, too frequent in colonies, they have taken
care to settle the price thereof at a moderate rate, by a general
tariff, which dispositions have appeared so wise and necessary
that His Majesty is resolved to favour the execution thereof;
and knowing that the exchanging of goods not being sufficient
to carry on commerce in its full extent, it is necessary in the
beginning of establishments of this nature, to give them all
possible protection and countenance, His Majesty is resolved
to supply the said company with a sum of bank bills, to enable
the inhabitants of Louisiana to trade amongst themselves,

and bring into France the fruits of their labour, industry and economy, without any risk or charge."

The effect of the deep interest taken by the Regent in the fortunes of the Company was twofold. It inspired confidence in the mind of the public at home. Of that and of its results special mention will require to be made. It also directed the eyes of suitable colonists to the new El Dorado, and set in motion a stream of emigration from the shores of France. Expeditions were fitted out by Law, and for these numerous vessels were both purchased and built. Everything was done on a scale in keeping with the dignity and magnitude of the Company. One of the pioneers, writing in 1721, has left on record an account of his experiences. The faintheartedness, however, which determined his speedy return, can hardly be attributed to his having been misled as to the character of the country, as he would wish us to believe, but rather to disappointment that the riches in quest of which he had gone could only be acquired by strenuous labour and after suffering many privations. "Our first embarkation for the Mississippi was at St. Malo; we were twelve ships, and carried with us agents, clerks, labourers, some troops, and provisions. After a tedious voyage, we arrived at Hispaniola, in the bay, and took Pensicola from the Spaniards on the Continent, being necessary for securing our navigation into the river, it lying almost at the mouth of it; the bay, which makes the mouth of the river Mississippi, is wider than from Orfordness to the North Foreland, and fuller of banks and shoals; so that it is very difficult for ships of any burthen to get into it, without very skilful pilots, of which there are none as yet; it hath three large openings, and one can hardly judge which is the mouth, though they all three come out of it, except by Monsieur d'Ibberville's Fort, which one hardly sees, till you are just upon it. After you have got into the river, it is still very shoal, though broad, till you get up to Monsieur d'Ibberville's second Fort, at both of which we are to begin our factories and carry them higher, as our people increases. Our Fort lies in about 28 degrees of latitude; the country is prodigiously sandy; and, I must say, they might as well have sent us to the deserts of Libia, or Barco, to have settled a colony, as thither; we met with no inhabitants near the sea-side, nor indeed for a great many leagues up the river; if you believe some people from Canada, that came to us, their navigation down this river was from 42 degrees to 28, directly south and north; the mountains, water-falls, on the way from Canada, and lakes are incredible; one lake, called Illinois, is so large, that they sailed 40 leagues over it. The different nations up the country, running along the back of the English plantations, I leave to others to describe, that is no part of my business; but the Iroquois, who we were told in France were the inhabitants, are not within a thousand miles of it, nor any other inhabitants. I saw for many hundred miles but here and there some straggling Indians, natives of Florida, and poor, innocent, harmless people. I went up the river in a canoe for some hundred of miles, without seeing the country mend, and after three months stay embarked again for France."

CHAPTER VI

CHAPTER VI

The Indian Company had only yet touched the fringe of the monopolies Law intended it to embrace. It had embarked upon a sea of dazzling speculation, but its journey was only at its commencement. Its destination, however, was by no means uncertain in the mind of the great financier, and this he was to reach in the space of four months.

The first great acquisition of value and importance was the transfer to the Company of the right of coinage. This was effected on the 25th of July, 1719. The right was to extend over a period of nine years, and the price was fixed at 50,000,000 livres, payable within fifteen months of the date of the grant. To place the Company in a position to carry out the bargain, a fresh issue of shares was made, and Law on this occasion took greater advantage of public enthusiasm than he did on the occasion of the previous issue. In the latter case the shares were offered at a premium of ten percent, the public, although paying 550 livres, receiving stock only of the value of 500 livres. In the present instance the 500 livres share was to be allotted on payment of 1000 livres, thus necessitating the issue of only 50,000 shares. In addition to enacting a premium, Law employed a device he had before resorted to. He made it a condition that subscribers should be already possessors of previously issued shares to the extent of five times more than the number of new shares they desired to have allotted to them. The effect of this was magical. The demand for old shares was so intense that they rose immediately to 2000 livres, and the rapidity of the rise only served to widen the circle of speculators. Law was thus bringing within his grasp practically the whole of the nation as participants in his schemes.

The universal enthusiasm, however, was not unmixed. The unaccustomed magnitude of Law's transactions was productive in certain quarters of considerable misgivings, and not a few were able amidst the general excitement to regard his schemes with more than usual calmness. Amongst those, of course, were found the financier's bitterest enemies. To discredit Law, and to baulk him in his efforts, they lost no opportunity; and to instill doubt in the public mind as to the sanity of their speculations was by no means a difficult task. It was only necessary to secure the support of a few in order to depress the value of the Mississippi stock. Extensive sales, ostensibly for the purpose of saving a further loss, but really for the purpose of undermining the market, produced in the following month a sharp reaction. The Earl of Stair writing to Secretary Craggs on the 20th of August, 1719, remarks in the course of his letter upon this sudden and disturbing attitude of the public. He says:

"Mississippi begins to stagger; the actions fall and there are no more buyers; which has happened by Law's imprudence, and boundless desire for gain. He had raised the actions to such a price that it required above forty millions to pay the interest at four percent. When the French, by degrees, began to make this calculation, and found that it was impossible that even the King could find his account to furnish such a sum annually to support Mississippi, they found themselves cheated; and they are now crowding to sell out. Law will do what he can to support the actions, but the thing is impossible. The mystery of the matter is this: in the original fund of one hundred millions, the King and the Regent had about forty millions; and the same proportion of additional subscription of fifty millions. The company bought the coinage of the King at fifty millions, to be paid in fifteen months. Besides these fifty millions, the King or the Regent, by selling out when the actions were at four hundred, might have got two hundred millions; at which rate they might have been supported. But by buoying them up to six hundred, to make the Regent win three hundred millions, Law risks to have the whole fabric tumble to the ground. For the French, who run on boldly and impetuously in the beginning of all enterprises, run back with the same impetuosity when once they are rebuffed. I do not know if I have explained this matter to you, so as that you will be able to understand. It is, certainly, something more extravagant and more ridiculous than anything that ever happened in any other country. I wish for your diversion I could but talk one hour to you upon that subject."

Law, however, was equal to the opposition of his enemies, and treated their efforts to undermine his position with the utmost indifference and contempt. He proceeded apace with the completion of his schemes, and was now approaching the zenith of his power. All that now remained for him to accomplish of his original plans was the purchase of the great farms and several other smaller sources of the national revenues.

The *anti-system* attempted by the brothers Paris, under the auspices of d'Argenson, had been carried out to the extent of a lease of the great revenue farms having been granted to Aymard Lambert, d'Argenson's valet-de-chambre, but had not been put into operation. Law now came forward and secured the lease on behalf of the Western Company, accomplishing the three-fold object of acquiring a valuable asset for the company, relieving the taxpayers from the intolerable exactions of the farmers, and, lastly, humiliating d'Argenson for the part he took in the *anti-system.* The grant of the great farms was formally made on the 27th, and of the other departments of taxation on the 31st of August. The treasury had derived from these sources the annual revenue of 48,000,000 livres, but Law offered a further sum of 3,500,000 livres for the privilege which was to extend over a period of nine years. The Company now declared its ability to pay a dividend of 200 livres upon its shares, or forty percent, upon its capital. Such a declaration at once counteracted the devices of Law's opponents to lower the price of the shares, and within a few days they rose to a premium of 1000 percent, at which extravagant price it was even extremely difficult to make substantial purchases. The demand was also created by the condition that allotment of the recently issued shares would only be in favour of those already possessed of stock. "The public," says Lord Stair, "has run upon this new subscription with that fury that near the double of that sum is subscribed for; and there have been the greatest brigues and quarrels to have place in the subscription, to that degree, that the new submissions are not yet delivered out, nor is the first payment received. Mr. Law's door is shut, and all the people of quality in France are on foot, in hundreds, before his door in the Place Vendôme."

Law now made the concluding proposal of his schemes. The absorption of *billets d'état* by the Company, although extensive, had not yet exhausted them. There still remained almost 1500 million livres in circulation, and Law was anxious to have them liquidated. He accordingly proposed to lend the king a sum of money sufficient for the purpose at three percent, per annum, and at the same time to reduce the interest upon the 100 millions previously advanced at four percent, to a similar rate; and in return for an offer so advantageous, he secured an extension of the various grants to the Company for the uniform period of fifty years. To carry through this, the largest and most important transaction upon which the Company had entered as yet, an issue of 300,000 new shares was made at a price of 5000 livres, thus yielding a premium of 4500 livres. These shares, however, were not to be allotted to the public. The Regent was fully alive to the possibility of enriching himself by securing the whole of the issue and profiting by the rise which would certainly take place in their value. He already was holder of 100,000 of previously issued shares, and of the whole capital of the company only 200,000 were in the hands of the public. The supply was accordingly unequal to the demand, and in the course of two months the shares reached the incredible price of 10,000 livres. A kind of madness had seized the nation. A royal road to fortune had been opened up by the ingenious foreigner; and had lured along its easy path an excited throng of princes and people, peers and commoners, clergy and laity, rich and poor in short all who by any means could hope to secure the coveted scrip. The memoirs of the period teem with instances of the excessive folly and rashness which characterised these halcyon days of the scheme, and display a want of balance on the part of the French nation entirely beyond belief.

That the public should thus have allowed their excitement of feelings to destroy their judgment so far as to ignore the primary elements of caution and of foresight can hardly be attributed to Law. No evidence can be brought of any intention on his part to utilize his financial genius for the purpose of blinding the nation to its own interests, and turning it merely to his own exclusive advantage. The effect of his schemes was entirely beyond his control. So far as the reception they would receive from the French nation was concerned, his own anticipations were only too clearly exceeded. He undoubtedly perceived the dangerous courses upon which the public had entered, but it would have been imprudent on his part to have endeavoured by any arbitrary act to check it. He firmly believed in the adequacy of his system to accomplish the objects which he stated he had in view. He may have been, and was, somewhat over-sanguine, but that was merely a fault of temperament, not a consequence of sinister motive. He may have been extravagant in praise of the possibilities of his schemes, but that was due to intensity of confidence in their efficacy, not to any deliberate intention to deceive.

The total capital of the company was now 300,000,000 livres, and to pay the promised dividend of 200 livres per share would require profits of at least 120,000,000 livres. Those profits were drawn principally from the interest payable by the State upon the advances made by the Company for the purposes of liquidating the national debt, from the coinage, from the tobacco monopoly, from the great farms, from the collection of general taxes, and from their general commerce. Amongst these, the only leakage which could occur would be in the latter, and Law's estimate of the profits derivable from it were placed at one-third of the whole. Such an estimate, however, may have been so wide of the mark that the expenditure incurred in the administration of the Company's commercial transactions might possibly have been so great as to absorb the whole of the surpluses accruing from the other departments. Time, however, could alone supply the test of this, but the downfall of the system anticipated the opportunity. Other contingencies arose, foreign to the business of the Company, which struck at its stability and brought its career to an unexpected end.

The closing months of 1719, and the opening months of 1720, saw the system at the height of its prosperity. Everything proceeded smoothly. Nothing ruffled the high hopes entertained by all as to its future. At the General Assembly of the proprietors of the Company held, on the 30th of December, 1719, for the purpose of communicating its position since the previous assembly, and of submitting the accounts for this year, it was reported that, although an accurate balance could not be struck owing to the overwhelming duties of the directors in carrying through the extensive negotiations of the previous months, "the proprietors may be assured that everything passes for the good and advantage of the Company; that the colonies of Louisiana are going on prosperously; that the trade to India, and that to Africa, and to the north, are assuming new vigour; that the produce of the Farms General is visible increasing; that there will be very considerable profits arising from the administration and striking of the coin and from the refining of the materials; that the Company wish to economize the expenses of taxations, and of the emoluments given to the Receivers General of Finance, so that the dividend of the old shares of the Western Company might be fixed at present at the proportion of forty percent, and a like dividend for the hundred and fifty millions of the new shares in the India Company."

The board of directors consisted of thirty members, each of whom was obliged to deposit 200 shares as security for his good administration. Their salaries were originally fixed at 6000 livres, but at the same meeting were increased to 30,000 livres, by no means an exorbitant sum in view of the magnitude of their labours and the greatness of their responsibility.

Interesting as had been the progress of the Company during the past year, the Bank which Law had founded had also undergone a great and momentous change. Since its institution in May, 1716, its operations had met with great success, and had secured the utmost confidence of the public, not only because of the soundness of the principles which dominated its administration, but also because of its careful and cautious management. The currency became more stable than it hitherto had been, and foreign trade developed where before it had been impossible by reason of the great uncertainty of the rates of exchange. The Regent, influenced by its success and labouring under the idea that this success could be permanently maintained even though its principal features were radically changed, determined to take control of Law's bank, and convert it from a private into a royal institution. Accordingly, on the 4th of December, 1718, the General Bank of Law and Company was proclaimed a Royal Bank, to be administered in future by the King and his advisers. This change was opposed by Law, who, knowing the character of the Regent, foresaw the possibility of disastrous results, but the Duc d'Orléans had decided upon the step, and opposition was of no avail. The new ordinance was to come into force on the 1st of January, 1719. The King reimbursed in specie the holders of the shares, and guaranteed the due payment of the notes in circulation which at that date amounted to 59,000,000 livres. The proprietors, who had, as already seen, only paid one fourth of their holding in specie and the remaining three fourths in depreciated *billets d'état* thus realised their investment in cash to the face value of their securities. Law was appointed Director-General of the Bank, acting under the instructions of the King through the Regent. Thus the King by this change became the sole proprietor of the Bank, and the dignity he conferred upon it secured it even more, if that were possible, in the good favour of his people.

It has already been stated that the notes of the General Bank were always convertible at sight into coin of the weight and standard of the day of issue, and that here lay its strength and security. The Regent, however, in all probability unwilling to restrict himself from taking advantage of depreciating the coinage at any time a favourable opportunity should present itself, divested the notes of the Bank of this excellent feature, and in the future they bore that. "The Bank promises to pay the bearer, at sight,—livres in silver coin, value received." This change, also opposed by Law, struck at the very root principle of good credit. It endeavoured to make paper the standard of currency, while no guarantee was given that the coinage would remain of a fixed and unvarying value. No legislative decree, no royal proclamation, can place an artificial value upon the medium of currency, unless there is also present the indispensable element of public confidence. A paper currency can only circulate at its nominal value if there is behind it the security of a fixed coinage and a fund of specie in reserve for conversion. The Regent in issuing his new notes offered neither of these, but on account of the favour into which the Bank had been brought by Law, the confidence of the public remained as yet at least unshaken. We will see, however, at a later stage the consequences which this disastrous change involved.

A further important step in the development of the Bank was the establishment of branches in the five important centres—Lyons, La Rochelle, Tours, Orléans, and Amiens. Those towns, which enjoyed the privilege of local parliaments such as Toulouse, Bordeaux, Rouen, Grenoble, Dijon and Metz, were carefully avoided by the Regent, who anticipated that the extension of the Bank to them might provoke unpleasant opposition. Other towns, again, where no provincial parliaments existed to consult, had otherwise displayed hostility to the Bank, and these also were not honoured by the presence of its branches. "Lisle, Marseilles, Nantz, Saint Malo, and Bayonne, were distinguished by this prudent exclusion." At the same time it was decreed that where branches of the Bank existed specie should only be legal tender up to 600 livres, notes being necessary for amounts beyond that sum, and that gold and silver were on no account, unless by special permission of the Bank authorities, to be transmitted to such towns. By these restrictions it was hoped that specie as a medium of currency would fall into desuetude and notes alone become recognised for purposes of exchange. This hope was expressed in the decree of the 22nd of April, 1719, which authorised the issue of 100,000,000 additional notes. "These cannot be subject to any diminution, as the specie is, inasmuch as the circulation of the Bank bills is more useful to the subjects of his Majesty, than that of the specie of gold and silver, and that they deserve a particular protection, in preference to the coin made of materials brought from foreign countries."

Before the close of the year, fresh issues were made to the extent of 900,000,000 livres; and on the 21st of December, silver and gold suffered further restriction as tender, the former being limited to ten livres and the latter to three hundred. The purpose of this was to force a paper currency, and as far as possible discourage the use of specie. By reducing to so low a limit the tender of gold and silver, a demand was created for the notes of the Bank, and very shortly the Bank had attracted to itself a large proportion of the coinage then in currency. People "ran there in crowds, conjuring and imploring the clerks to receive their specie, and thinking themselves happy when they succeeded. Upon which, a merry fellow wittily called out to those who were the most forward; 'Don't be afraid, gentlemen, that your money should remain on your hands; it shall all be taken from you.'"

The effect was to a large extent as the Regent had wished. Paper circulated with the greatest freedom, and the highly speculative mood in which the people indulged was productive of an appearance of peculiarly false prosperity. Money as represented in notes became exceedingly abundant because of the manner in which it was distributed. Everyone spent with a lavish hand, regardless of the possibility of Law's schemes receiving a sudden and unexpected check, thus bringing about a dislocation of the supply of money. Luxuries became necessaries, and domestic life displayed the grossest degrees of unbridled extravagance. To supply the great demand for rich cloths, costly furniture, and all the various luxuries which only find a ready market when prosperity spreads over a whole community, new industries arose throughout the country, and labour not only became scarce but was able to command in some cases four times its previous value. A taste arose too for works of art, and the best of the continent was sent into France where fabulous prices were obtained with a readiness proportionate to the ease with which the fortunes of the investors were made. Duhautchamp, in his *History of the Scheme*, gives several instances of this extravagance on the part of the nouveaux riches. Of one he says that, "He carried his magnificence so far, that most of the deeds related of him appear fabulous. His hotel in Paris, his gardens, his furniture, his equipage, the number of his servants of all degrees and professions, equalled those of the greatest princes. A certain jeweller declares that he supplied him with more than three millions worth of precious stones, without reckoning the beautiful diamond of the Count de Nocé for which he paid 500,000 livres, and a girdle buckle which a Jew sold him for the same sum. With regard to his furniture, being a connoisseur of good taste, he had selected the whole so well, that, to form an idea of the magnificence of his apartments, we must have recourse to descriptions which are used of fairy palaces. Not content with 4000 marcs of silver and silver gilt service which he had first ordered, he found means to carry off from the jeweller's that which had been made for the King of Portugal, under pretext that the agents of that prince had been wanting in punctuality of payment. Besides this magnificent table service, he furnished himself with stands, mirrors, braziers, orange-tree cases, flower pots, etc. Lastly all his cooking utensils were of silver. As for his upholstery, he took everything which could be imagined of that kind that was most precious. He had no less than eighty horses in his stables his equipages equalled in number those of the grand Sultan. The number of his servants was nearly ninety, amongst whom were comprised intendant, secretaries, steward, surgeon, valets-de-chambre, upholsterers, four young ladies as chamber maids, and for his grooms four footmen of birth very superior to that of their master. Even when he went to dine away from home, he had his own table served as sumptuously as if he were present. It was served with everything most exquisite, principally during the year 1720. He was supplied with young peas which had cost 100 pistoles the pint. Nothing was wanting that the most voluptuous gourmet could think of. The desserts that were served were fitted to surprise the most expert mechanicians. Large fruits, which would have deceived the eyes of the most clear sighted, were so artistically contrived that when anyone, surprised at seeing a beautiful melon in winter, attempted to touch it, he caused a number of little fountains to spring up of different sorts of spirituous liquors which delighted the sense of smell, whilst the master of the house, pressing his foot on a concealed spring, made an artificial figure walk round the table and pour out nectar to the ladies, before whom he was made to stop. In a word, I doubt whether the famous feasts of Antony and Augusta, so vaunted in history, had anything more rare than those which our fortunate millionaire took a pleasure in giving."

CHAPTER VII

Hotel Mazarin acquired as office of Company and of Bank—Excitement of crowds in the Rue Vivienne and the Rue Quincampoix—Curious sources of fortune—Instances of enormous fortunes acquired by members of the nobility—Enormous influx of foreign speculators into Paris.

CHAPTER VII

In order that the Company and the Bank might be housed in a style of magnificence befitting the brilliance of their careers, the Hotel Mazarin had been purchased at a cost of one million livres. Both were now under one roof, and Law was thus enabled to devote himself, with greater ease and less inconvenience, to their management. This was all the more necessary since the Bank and the Company, although nominally distinct and separate undertakings carrying on different classes of business, were yet in reality part and parcel of the same system, engaged in accomplishing the same ultimate objects and working in co-operation in all their transactions. Of both, Law was the controlling spirit. The Bank, now the property of the Crown, was placed entirely under the management of its founder upon whom no restrictions were laid, and the Company although under the directorate of thirty proprietors was equally in his hands. Their will was invariably his wish, and in everything they yielded with ready compliance to the suggestions of the great financial genius.

While the Hotel Mazarin was the centre from which the fuel for the prevailing excitement was distributed, its intensity was only really felt and displayed in another quarter. When the day of issue of shares arrived, the Rue Vivienne in which the Company's offices were situated, and all the adjoining streets and squares, were crowded by speculators of all degrees. Unseemly rushes took place amongst the throng. Each one regarded his neighbour as a rival for the possession of the coveted scrip, and crushed and jostled himself though the crowd towards the enchanted building so that he might be amongst the first to enter when its doors were opened to hand over the shares to successful applicants. Lemontey compared them to a phalanx which "advanced for several days and nights towards the Exchange office, like a compact column, which neither sleep, hunger, nor thirst could destroy. But at the fatal cry which announced the delivery of the last share, the whole vanished at once." So great was the number of applicants that on several occasions considerable difficulty and delay were experienced in compiling the lists of allottees. Public patience at these times was thoroughly exhausted, and gave way to frantic disorder and not infrequently to scenes of violence. The aristocracy, in order that they might not be compelled to mix with the crowds on the street in their patient wait to know the result of their efforts to secure allotment, rented rooms and houses in the Rue Vivienne, and so great was the demand for accommodation that fortunate proprietors were in a position to charge the most exorbitant rates.

The excitement and frenzy however reached its highest point in the Rue Quincampoix. Here was the Stock Exchange of the day. A short narrow street of fifty yards in length and two or three in breadth, it ran from the Rue aux Ours to the Rue Aubry-le-Boucher, and contained the offices and houses of the bankers of the period. So confined was it that the crowds of speculators entirely blocked it as a thoroughfare, and drivers were prohibited from making use of it. Gates were erected at each end, and guards with drums were stationed to inform people when the street was opened or closed for business. Other restrictions were imposed upon the use of the street. The entrance by the Rue Aubry-le-Boucher was reserved for members of the aristocracy, and that by the Rue aux Ours for all others, but inside the gates no distinction of rank was respected. On Sundays and fête days the street was closed altogether, and in order that business might not proceed to hours which would disturb the rest of those who resided in the neighbourhood, the guards were ordered to clear the speculators from the street at a reasonable hour in the evening.

As in the case of the tenants and proprietors of houses in the Rue Vivienne, opportunity to even greater extent was afforded those who resided in the Rue Quincampoix to let their houses as dwellings or offices to the infatuated crowd of speculators. A house for which a rent of eight hundred livres per annum was paid secured without difficulty for its occupier a return of 5000 to 12,000 livres per month, single rooms in many cases returning as much as 1500 livres per month. Fortunes were made by many people who anticipated the demand for accommodation and secured a number of houses at little above their normal rent for the purpose of letting at these extravagant figures. Curious, too, were the methods adopted by some for the making of money. We read of a hunchback who converted his deformity to the original and profitable use of a writing desk. In a very few days he had accumulated the sum of 150,000 livres from the fees he received from the speculators who took advantage of the novel purpose to which he put his hunch. The same eccentric occupation enabled a soldier, possessed of very broad shoulders, to obtain his discharge from the army and purchase an estate in the provinces to which he prudently retired before the fever of speculation had enthralled him. We read too of a cobbler who plied his trade in a very primitive manner under four planks secured to a wall. The crowds of ladies who were drawn to the Rue Quincampoix as interested spectators in its exciting scenes suggested to the cobbler the means of gaining in a short time more than the labour of a lifetime could secure for him. He furnished his diminutive stall with chairs, and these he let out to ladies at exorbitant charges gladly paid. He then added to his stock a supply of pens and paper which were taken advantage of by brokers and others who resorted to his stall to carry out their transactions. By these means he drew an income of 50,000 livres per month.

However, these and other similar methods of acquiring fortunes were only incidental to the main business of the Rue Quincampoix. Great and unexpected fortunes were made by speculators in the Company's shares, and these by no means were confined to the wealthy capitalists or even persons possessed of moderate sums available for operation. The methods provided for exchange were of the crudest description, and provided means of amassing wealth for those who were absolutely without capital but were unscrupulous enough to take advantage of the opportunities that were opened up to them. Innumerable instances are recorded where servants, the most menial, enriched themselves in this way. One shareholder desirous of disposing his holding was too unwell to carry out the sale himself and sent his servant to carry through the transaction. He was instructed to sell two hundred and fifty shares at 8000 livres per share. On arrival at the Rue Quincampoix, he found the shares had meanwhile risen to 10,000 livres. The difference of 500,000 livres he retained, and with it speculated further until he succeeded in multiplying it four times, when he retired from the scene of his good fortune to enjoy the fruits of his ill-earned money. Another, who had been entrusted with the realisation of two hundred shares, took advantage of the rapidly rising market to postpone the disposal of them until the price enabled him to obtain 1,000,000 livres beyond their value on the day upon which they were handed to him, and this he regarded as his own, only paying to his principal the price they would have brought had they been immediately realised.

Amusing too, are many of the stories of those who found themselves so suddenly raised from extreme indigence to excess of wealth. Carriages thronged the streets whose occupants were formerly coachmen and footmen, cooks and scullery-maids, butlers and valets. A footman who had established himself in a palatial residence betrayed his former station by mounting behind his own carriage instead of entering it, and when reminded of his mistake excused himself by the remark that he wished to engage more footmen, and desired to know if there were room for them. Another footman, according to the Regent's mother, was in the habit of doing the same thing, but in his case intentionally, in order that he might the more experience the pleasure of the change his newly gained wealth had brought to him. Amongst menials none were more fortunate than those who were in attendance on Law himself. It is said that his coachman, having made for himself a competency, desired to leave the financier's service, and on expressing his desire to Law was allowed to do so on condition that he provided a substitute. This was naturally easily complied with, and in a short time he returned with two suitable men, of whom he offered one to Law, mentioning that he intended retaining the other for himself.

It was, however, amongst the higher ranks of society that the greatest scramble for wealth took place, and amongst the entourage of the court that the deepest gambling in shares was indulged in. Peers, court favourites, ladies of fashion, judges, bishops, and practically everyone of standing in society or in the public service, were to be found day after day in the Rue Quincampoix, engaged in the purchase and sale of the Mississippi stock. The Regent himself was one of the most successful participants in the national gamble, and with princely and lavish generosity, marked his sudden and easy access of enormous wealth. Amongst charitable institutions he distributed several million livres, giving in particular one million each to the Hotel-Dieu, the Hospital General, and the Foundlings. The debts of prisoners to the extent of one and a half millions were discharged, and to many of his friends he gave gifts of varying, but extravagant, amounts. The Marquis de Nocé, the Count de la Motte, and the Count de Roie, were each recipients of 100,000 livres, and the Count de la Marche, a child of thirteen years, son of the Prince de Conti, had conferred upon him a pension of 60,000 livres. He also increased by 130,000 livres, the pension enjoyed by his mother, the Princess Palatine, who wrote in her letters that "we hear nothing but millions spoken of now; my son has given me two millions in shares, which I have distributed among my household. The King has also taken some millions for his household. All the royal household have received some, all the children of France, the grandchildren of France, and the Princes of the blood."

The Duke of Bourbon, son of Louis XIV and Madame de Montespan, repaired his broken fortunes, liquidated his enormous debts, and in the course of several successful strokes of speculation, acquired a fortune of twenty million livres. He purchased large estates in Picardy, and acquired all the most valuable land between the Oise and the Somme. The castle at Chantilly was rebuilt on a scale of regal magnificence, and an extensive zoological collection was brought together as a feature of attraction to his territorial possessions. Anxious to improve the breed of horses in France, he also imported 150 racehorses from England, and thus established one of the finest stables on the continent of Europe. And then, "to pay his court to the Regent, who was passionately fond of his daughter, the Duchess of Berry, he gave that Princess, who was eager after pleasure, a superb festival, which lasted four or five days, and cost an immense sum of money."

Among other nobles whose dilapidated fortunes were restored at this time, were the Dukes d'Antin, de Guiche, de la Force, the Marshal d'Estrées, Madame de Vérue and the Princes de Rohan and de Poix. But many foreigners were no less successful, and of one, Joseph Gage, brother of Viscount Gage, who had acquired an exceedingly large fortune, we are told that, having aspirations to kingly rank, he offered the King of Poland three millions if the latter would resign his crown in his favour, and meeting with an unfavourable reply, endeavoured to negotiate a similar transaction with reference to Sardinia, but with no greater success.

Fortune, however, did not shine on all the members of the nobility of France. Many were unable or unwilling to take advantage of the opportunities offered them for enrichment. Of the latter the most conspicuous were Chancellor d'Aguessau, the Duc de Saint-Simon, the Duc de la Rochefoucauld, Marshal de Villeroy and Marshall de Villars. For the former, other means were discovered for acquiring wealth than direct speculation, means less creditable, if not more discreditable. The institution of marriage was utilized by the poor nobility to replenish their finances. Many of the nouveaux riches were only too pleased to endow a prospective noble son-in-law with wealth sufficient to enable him to live according to his station, so that they too might be able to number themselves among the aristocracy. Until the advent of Law, marriages of this kind were not only unusual, but so strict was the line of division which separated the nobility from all inferior ranks, that when they were celebrated, they invariably brought social ostracism. The charms of wealth, however, removed all scruples of caste, and we find, for instance, that the marriage of Mlle. de Sainte-Hermine, a near relation of the Duc de la Vrilliere, Secretary of State, whose consent was willingly given, to a parvenu of the name of Panier, was celebrated without any reflection on the ground of misalliance. But marriages of a very different class from these were brought into favour amongst this class of suitor during these days of financial excitement. These were known as marriages à réméré,—marriages with right of redemption, the distinctive feature of which consisted in the right of the noble husband to cancel the marriage at a future date. Marais instances the case of the Marquis d'Oise, of the house of Villars-Brancas, who entered into a proposal of marriage with a little girl of two years old, daughter of André the Mississippian. The betrothal was made with the consent of the two families. The Marquis was to have an annuity of 20,000 livres until the marriage took place, and even in case it never took place. If it took place, the dowry was to be four millions. Little girls would no longer have dolls, but asked for "Marquises of Oise to play with."

This marriage, however, did not take place, the pretext for its cancellation being found in the subsequent fall of André on the collapse of the scheme. The marriage of the Count d'Evreux was of the same class. His wife was a young girl of twelve, daughter of the famous Crozat. The Count received a sum of 2,000,000 livres on the marriage, but, subsequently gaining enormous profits on successful share transactions, repaid the dowry and obtained release from the nuptial tie.

During these months of excitement, Paris was a centre of an attraction equally for the foreigner as for the Frenchman. The brilliance of the capital was dazzling, and the facilities for spending money were even greater than those for making it. The influx was from all nations and drawn from every grade. The sovereigns even of foreign countries did not disdain to engage in the general business of share speculation, and sent to Paris specially appointed agents for the purpose, or made use of their ministers already at the French court. Britain too supplied its quota of speculators. The Earl of Ilay, a friend of Law's, and anxious to benefit his friends at home by turning his friendship to account, in writing to Mrs. Howard in Sept., 1719, said, "I have laid out the money you bid me. It is very difficult in a letter to give you an idea of the funds of this country; but in fact everybody has made estates that have been concerned in them for four or five months. As a little instance of this, cousin Jack has got, I believe, near; £10,000, and has lost the half of that sum by a timorous silly bargain he made; for my part, I came after all was in a manner over, and as I never meddle with these matters, I do nothing but buy books and gimcracks. It is true it is now very late, and yet, by what I am informed by him who knows all, and does all, I am of opinion that whatever sum you remit here may be turned to great profit. The stocks are now at 950, and if no accidents happen of mortality, it is probable they will be 1500 in a short time. The money I laid out for you was 5000 livres, as a subscriber to the fifty millions of stock lately added, of which the tenth part only is paid down, so that 5000 is the first payment of 50,000 livres. The subscription was full, but Mr. Law was so kind as to allow it me; some of the subscribers have already sold their subscriptions for 230, that is their own money back again and 130 percent, profit Whatever you think fit to do, you may bid Middleton remit to me as many livres. I shall acknowledge the receipt of them and do the best I can. You will think that the levity of this country has turned my head when I tell you your master might, within these few months, have made himself richer than his father."

It was estimated that at the end of 1719, no fewer than 305,000 foreigners were in Paris, drawn there in the hope of securing immediate wealth. So large an accession to the population had the effect of stimulating business. Housing accommodation became exceedingly scarce, and every available out-house was utilised as a temporary place of abode. Not only did the necessaries of life rise greatly in price, but all articles of luxury shared in the general increase of value. The effect was to create an appearance of great prosperity which permeated every class of the community, and elicited expressions of deep respect and admiration for the man who had inaugurated this new era of apparent greatness for France.

CHAPTER VIII

Law's importance causes him to be courted by all classes—
Socially ostracised by nobility—Law's conversion to Roman
Catholicism—Role of the Abbé Dubois and the Abbé Tencin
in the conversion—Difficulties in its accomplishment—Law
becomes naturalized—Law appointed Comptroller-General
of Finance—Regent celebrates appointment by a distribution
of pensions—Law honoured with the freedom of the City of
Edinburgh—Law Elected member of Academy of Sciences—
William Law brought to France and made Postmaster-
General—Law's private investments—His fiscal reforms—His
introduction of free university education.

CHAPTER VIII

In the midst of all this excitement, gaiety and brilliance, Law himself stood out as the one great and prominent figure in the kingdom. Court was paid to him by all the most influential personages in France; and by the multitude he was regarded with feelings of awe and admiration. His chambers were crowded day after day by those who at other times would have been in attendance upon their sovereign. Every excuse and artifice was employed in order to obtain an interview with the great man. "I have seen an hundred coaches at his levee in a morning, and dukes and peers waiting for hours together to speak with him, and could not get within two rooms of him for the crowd." Yet through the whole of this period of flattery and adulation he maintained the same cool unaffected demeanour which had always characterised him, and although given at times to treat his importunate visitors with haughtiness and curtness, yet he was noted for his general suavity and affability when receiving those who were strangers to him, and who had sought introductions without credentials merely for the purpose of obtaining pecuniary assistance. When he passed along the streets, he was followed by crowds by whom he was greeted with cries of "Long live Mr. Law." Ladies of the highest rank kissed their hands to him, and even princes rendered him obeisance in public. In fact, so important had Law become in the eyes of everyone, that he allowed himself to indulge in conduct of a somewhat shameless character, although it was attributed simply to boldness by those who encouraged him in it. The latter—and they were more often than not of the gentler sex—thought they excused their conduct in endeavouring to give it the character of a joke, and the nobility of the period, ready at all times to sacrifice their lives to their honour, scrupled not to sacrifice their honour to their fortune.

The determination of many ladies to have the honour, as they considered it, of speaking with Law, led to many amusing if not ridiculous incidents. One lady, who had waited without success at his house for an interview, instructed her coachman to overturn her carriage if on any occasion when driving her he chanced to meet the great financier. For several days she drove through the streets of Paris he was most in the habit of frequenting, and at last her patience was rewarded. On the approach of Law her coachman upset the carriage, and the lady who was carried into a neighbouring house by the object of her attentions confessed the purpose of her stratagem, and extracted a promise from him that her application for shares would be granted. Not so successful, however, was the ruse of another lady who had failed to secure an invitation to the house of Madame de Simiane where Law was to dine. Driving to the house when all were seated at dinner, she bade her coachman and footman to shout "Fire," at which the guests all rushed into the street. On seeing the lady leave her carriage to meet him, Law at once perceived the object of the false alarm and fled before she had an opportunity of speaking to him.

At Law's house was always to be found the most exclusive society in Paris, and it is related that the Regent, expressing the desire on one occasion to find a duchess to whom he could depute the duty of accompanying his daughter to Modena, mentioned to the Abbé Dubois that he did not exactly know where to find one, to which the latter remarked, "I can tell you where to find every duchess in France: you have only to go to Mr. Law's; you will see them every one in his ante-chamber."

One incident, however, serves to show that there was no desire on the part of the nobility to admit Law to their ranks, and that their conduct in apparently placing him on their own social level was merely dictated by the possibility of utilising their friendship for financial gain. The Maréchal de Villeroy had arranged a ballet in which the young king was to appear. Such ballets had been common during the reign of Louis XIV, and were considered part of a nobleman's education, which then chiefly consisted in "grace, address, exercise, respect for bearing, graduated and delicate politeness, polished and decent gallantry," but had fallen entirely into disuse during the Regency. Great difficulty was accordingly experienced by the Maréchal in obtaining a sufficient number of dancers amongst the nobility who alone were formerly privileged to take part in the royal entertainment. Many were admitted who would not otherwise have been allowed to join in the ballet, and Law requested the Regent to obtain the honour for his son of being allowed to join the company. The Maréchal was unable to refuse the Regent's request, but the idea of a commoner's son occupying a place in a royal ballet so scandalised the feelings of social propriety of the privileged circle that "nothing else was spoken of for some days; tongues wagged freely, too; and a good deal of dirty water was thrown upon other dancers in the ballet." The success of the ballet was thus threatened, and the whole project promised to be a total failure when it was announced that Law's son had fallen ill from small-pox. The cause of all the difficulties having thus been removed, the high-born courtiers displayed their undisguised satisfaction and proceeded with calmer feelings to carry out the first and only Court ballet which graced the reign of Louis XV.

While Law's influence at this time was all-powerful in the government of France, he was without any of the outward symbols of authority. He held no office, and his influence accordingly could only be exercised indirectly. He enjoyed the splendour of the position to which he had attained, but did not possess any official mark of greatness. Two obstacles existed to official advancement. His religion was not that recognised by the State; and his nationality was foreign. Both of these he was now prepared to renounce. The abjuration of his religion was a step which required to be accomplished with the utmost caution. All the elements of sincerity were lacking, and Law's conversion was likely to be regarded as a merely political move. There was danger moreover of the public regarding the conversion of Law under royal auspices in the light of a highly scandalous proceeding, and considering that it might derogate from the high office to which he was destined and for which the abjuration of his religion was a necessary preliminary. There was a circumstance also in Law's career which under ordinary conditions would have militated against his admission to the Roman Catholic communion, and therefore required delicate treatment. Law had not been legally married to the lady whom he passed off as his wife, and the law of the Church strictly required cessation of all relations with her. This, naturally, was a course to which Law would not assent since by her he had a son and a daughter, and since her husband Senor was now dead for many years. It was accordingly necessary to have a very indulgent converter, one who would not only attest sincere conversion but would at the same time refrain from interfering with Law's connubial relations. An accommodating instrument had therefore to be found, and Dubois was ready to supply him in the person of a certain Abbé Tencin. "I shall give you," said Dubois, "neither a curé nor a habitué de paroisse: they are too much bound by formularies, maxims, and rigid rules; you will have the Abbé Tencin, a man of considerable talent whom I know intimately; he can convert and receive into the Church Mr. Law and all his family." The Abbé was undoubtedly a man of talent, ambitious and witty, but unfortunately had acquired a reputation for unscrupulousness, and a degree of dishonesty inconsistent with his high professions. Regarded with suspicion, and denied the friendship of those with whom his calling would have brought him into contact, he devoted himself to intriguing on behalf of politicians and others to whom a man of the ability and cunningness of the Abbé was indispensable. To Dubois he was invaluable, but he also had that minister under his control through his having compromised himself with Madame de Tencin. The Abbé found in this a powerful lever, and unfailingly turned it to his own advantage at every opportunity. Law's conversion was such an opportunity, and one which opened out a prospect of enrichment he had not as yet enjoyed.

With the approval of the Regent, the Abbé was accordingly deputed to perform the delicate task of making Law a Catholic. A short time was allowed to elapse before the actual ceremony took place, and in the interval it was supposed that Law, under the spiritual guidance of the Abbé, was preparing himself for the solemn and important step he was about to take. But by no ingenious form of deception, however mild, was the Abbé able to give even a colour of sincerity to Law's conversion, and he was therefore placed under the necessity of choosing some other place than Paris for the performance of the ceremony lest the people, outraged in their notions of religious propriety, should resort to forcible measures to prevent the ceremony from taking place. The Church of the Récollets in Melun was accordingly chosen as a sufficiently safe and retired scene for the abjuration, and on the 17th of September, 1719, the necessary formalities were performed, the Abbé retiring from "his pious task with

many shares and banknotes." The event was made the occasion
of sarcastic verse of which a few fragments still survive. The
following fragment preserved in the *Mémoris du Marshal Duc
de Richelieu* celebrates the bestowal of the title of Primate of the
Mississippi upon the Abbé by the Colonel of the Regiment of
Skull-Caps, a burlesque association which jested on all events:

> *Nous Colonel de la Calotte,*
> *Pour empêcher par tous moyens,*
> *Que l'erreur des Luthériens*
> *Et que la Doctrine Huguenotte*
> *N'infecte notre Régiment*
> *D'un pernicieux sentiment;*
> *Et pour mettre dans la voye,*
> *Quiconque seroit fourvoy,*
> *Et seroit devenu la proye*
> *De l'Hérétique Devoyé.*
> *A ces causes, vu la science,*
> *Bonnes moeurs, doctrine, éloquence*
> *Et zele que l'Abbé Tencin*
> *A fait paroître sur-tout autre;*
> *Pour le salut de son prochain,*
> *Nous lui donnons Lettre d'Apôtres,*
> *Et de convertisseur en chef;*
> *D'autant qu'en homme apostolique,*
> *Il a rendu Law Catholique:*
> *En outre par le même bref,*
> *Voulant illustrer la soutane,*
> *Et donner du poids aux Sermons*
> *Dudit Abbé; nous le nommons*
> *Primat de la Louisiane.*
> *De plus, quoique l'Abbé susdit,*
> *Plein d'un évangélique esprit,*

Meprise les biens de ce monde,
Et que même contre eux il fronde.
De notre libéralité
Pour soutenir sa dignité,
En conséquence du systême
Lui déléguons dîme on dixieme
Sur les brouillards dudit pays,
Qui du systême sont le prix;
Espérant qui la Cour de Rome
Donnera les Bulles gratis.

An unexpected difficulty, however, now arose. Law's parish church was the church of Saint-Roch, and the Curé, refusing to credit the sincerity of the conversion, would not recognize Law as a duly converted Catholic. This was a serious difficulty since Law had renounced his old faith and, while having complied with all the outward formalities necessary for reception into the new, was denied admission. The realisation of his ambition was thus threatened, and the situation demanded the employment of measures, extreme if necessary, but sufficient at least to overcome the scruples of the recalcitrant Curé. Tencin, as intermediary in the negotiations which followed, had full and ample powers to treat with the Curé. The wily Abbé, knowing that corruption was closed to him as an avenue of successful approach to the Curé, adopted the useful method, but one none the less corrupt because it does not personally benefit the recipient, of offering on behalf of his principal to subscribe lavishly to the funds of the church, and to give substantial assistance towards its construction. The Curé yielded readily to the temptation, and it was thereupon arranged that Law should communicate and make the bread offering at High Mass on Christmas Day with all due solemnity, His donations were attributed to a sense of religious duty, and as a thank-offering for the privilege of being received into the Catholic communion. The ceremony was performed before a crowded and fashionable congregation, who had flocked from Paris to witness the interesting event, and Law was now able to take out letters of naturalisation.

Law, however, was not permitted to escape so easily from public reflection upon the apparent motives of his action. A heated controversy arose between Jansenites, who, influenced only by rigid principle, were indignant at the manner in which a sacred rite had been in their opinion grossly abused, and the Jesuits, who, inclined to place more weight upon outward ceremony, were convinced, or at least declared they were convinced, of the sincerity of the conversion. Nor were matters improved when during the controversy all the compromising features of Law's past life were diligently gathered and as diligently published to a curious and interested community.

But Law chose to treat the matter in a spirit of indifference, and by refraining from making any attempt to refute or explain the statements of his opponents the storm subsided from mere exhaustion.

A few days after the ceremony at Saint-Roch, on the 5th of January, 1720, Law was named Comptroller-General of Finance in place of d'Argenson, whose tenure of office was wholly at Law's mercy. Law had merely to create difficulties for his nominee, in order to obtain his resignation, and d'Argenson wise enough to perceive the futility of opposing the designs of Law readily yielded up the most important office in the national administration. As Voltaire remarks, Law had in the space of four years developed from a Scotsman into a Frenchman; from a Protestant into a Catholic; from an adventurer into a lord of the fairest lands of the kingdom; and from a banker into a minister of state. His phenomenal rise from obscurity to the highest office, and that in a foreign country, was an apparent witness to the truth of his theories, and the circumstance that he did not allow himself to be overcome by overestimation of his own importance, but maintained an unassuming and unpretentious manner throughout the whole of this period secured for him the personal attachment and admiration of the whole nation, and for his opinions a greater degree of implicit faith than probably they would otherwise have received.

The Regent was himself delighted with the preferment he was thus easily enabled to confer upon his favourite, and marked the occasion by a lavish distribution of grants and pensions to numerous courtiers and relations. Of these the Duke of Saint-Simon mentions grants of 600,000 livres to La Fare, captain of the guard; 100,000 livres to Castries, chevalier d'honneur to Madame la Duchesse d'Orléans; 200,000 to the Prince de Courtenay; and 60,000 livres to the Comte de la Marche, the infant son of the Prince de Conti. Saint-Simon then adds that "seeing so much depredation, and no recovery to hope for, I asked M. la Duc d'Orléans to attach 12,000 livres, by way of increase, to my government of Senlis, which was worth only 1000 livres, and of which my second son had the reversion. I obtained it at once."

Two other honours of a different character were also conferred upon Law during these few months of greatness. One came from his native city, which was now anxious to do homage to the man of whom it formerly had reason to be somewhat ashamed. This consisted of the freedom of Edinburgh, presented to him in a gold casket of magnificent workmanship, which had cost the municipal treasury the sum of £300. The other consisted in his election as an honorary member of the Academy of Sciences, an honour of the highest order and conferred only upon Frenchmen of outstanding ability. In this latter condition was found the excuse for purging his name from the roll on his downfall, his election which took place on the 2nd of December, 1719, having preceded his naturalisation.

The magnitude and diversity of interests to which Law's time and attention was now devoted were such as to cause him to enlist the services of his brother, William Law, a man of parts but much inferior in ability to his more brilliant brother. William Law was first appointed representative of the Bank on the London Exchange, and so great was the standing of the Bank in the opinion of English commercial circles that the bulk of remittances for France passed through his hands. His business capacity, however, was such as to warrant Law in bringing his brother over to Paris, and accordingly a London office was established in the Strand under the management of one George Middleton. Before setting out for Paris, William Law had made arrangements for the importation into France of considerable numbers of skilled workmen, chiefly gold and silver smiths. It had always been one of Law's objects to develop France into a great industrial nation, and one of the methods he adopted to accomplish this end was to rob England of its best workmen by offering substantial inducements. A factory was established at Versailles in which it was intended to carry on, on a large scale, a business which would gradually absorb certain classes of trade that had hitherto been practically the monopoly of British manufacturers. Success however did not come as Law had anticipated. No doubt his efforts were a stimulating influence, but he was to discover that trade, which was not of natural growth, seldom prospered by purely artificial means.

William Law on his arrival in Paris was received with that welcome which his relationship with the Comptroller-General naturally secured for him. He was introduced immediately to the Regent, and was not only made one of the directors of the Bank, but was also appointed to the office of Postmaster-General a circumstance which alone indicates the commanding influence Law exercised over the Regent and the government of France. These two brothers lived in princely fashion in

Paris, honoured and courted by everyone from the Regent downwards. Each accumulated enormous wealth, but directed its investment into different, channels. William purchased land and estates in his native country, not that he foresaw the possibility of the collapse of his brother's schemes, but because he had no desire to permanently settle in France. John, on the other hand, with the intention of becoming a Frenchman so far as that was possible in spite of his origin, acquired great estates throughout the land of his adoption, and thus incidentally evinced his confidence in the sterling value of his financial schemes. His nephew compiled a list of his more important investments, aggregating almost 8,000,000 livres:

Enumeration of the Purchases of John Law

	Livres
Le Marquisat d'Effiat (en Auvergne)	800,000
La Terre de la Riviere	900,000
Le Marquisat de Toucy	160,000
La Terre de la Marche	120,000
La Terre de Roissy	650,000
La Terre d'Orcher	400,000
Terre et Bois de Brean	160,000
Marquisats de Charleville et Bacqueville	330,000
La Terre de Berville	200,000
La Terre de Fontaine Rome	130,000
La Terre de Serville	110,000
La Terre d'Yville	200,000
La Terre de Gerponville	220,000
La Terre de Tancarville (en Normandie)	320,000
La Terre de Guermande	160,000
Hotel Mazarin, et Emplacemens Rue Vivienne	1,200,000
Emplacemens Rue de Varenne	110,000

Emplacemens de la Place Louis le Grand	250,000
Partie du fief de la Grange Batelière	150,000
Marais ou Chantiers du Fauxbourg St. Honore	160,000
Maisons, surtout dans Paris	700,000
Les Domains de Bourget	90,000
Quelques petites terres, comme Valançay, St. Suplice, etc.	350,000

	7,870,000

Not by any means a strikingly large list for the man who had in so few years enabled the Regent and innumerable members of the aristocracy to accumulate vast wealth and rehabilitate the fortunes which successive generations had squandered in reckless extravagance.

That Law did not merely use the great power and influence he had acquired in the government of France for the purpose of promoting his own financial schemes and his own personal advantage is evident from the radical reforms he accomplished in the fiscal arrangements of that country. The principles upon which he based his fiscal policy were of the most advanced and enlightened character. They were liberal, and consequently had strict equality for their object. The system of taxation which prevailed not only showed many anomalies but lent itself to the grossest abuse. Monopolies of every description abounded. Officials swarmed throughout the country, and by their extortionate levies upon every branch of trade checked industrial progress in every direction. It is said that in Paris itself the number of officials equalled the number of people engaged in the various trades they were supposed to supervise in the interests of the nation. Free trading intercourse was also limited by the existence of a system of provincial protection which sought to prevent the goods of one province from entering, except under payment of prohibitive dues, the markets of another province.

Law was alive to the prejudicial effects of all these factors upon the industrial prosperity of the country, and also upon the general well-being of the people, and endeavoured as far as possible to remove or at least to modify them. His ideal was the adoption of a single tax to be levied in proportion to the wealth of the individual. Too many vested interests existed however for the accomplishment of so sweeping a reform, and he had to satisfy himself with measures more moderate in their sweep. It is a tribute to his fearlessness that during the winter of 1719-20 he introduced innumerable changes in the method and incidence of taxation, and that in spite of the overwhelming opposition of those who were thus deprived of continuing the old extortionate system to their own pecuniary gain. By wholesale modification of duties and charges, he succeeded in effecting substantial reductions in the price of such necessaries as grain, corn, coal, wood, butter, cheese, and eggs. Inland protective duties were abolished on all articles classed as necessaries or as raw material, and on one item of import English coal the tariff was removed for the benefit of French manufacturers, whom Law was most anxious to encourage.

But Law's horizon was not bounded by the commercial and industrial interests of the country. He recognised the great part which education plays in the progress of a nation, and determined to give such facilities as would place the highest education within the reach of every one. He accordingly appropriated a twenty-eighth part of the postal revenue for the endowment of free education in the University of Paris. He thus conferred upon France a benefit of the most invaluable character, and by this measure alone merited the reputation of an enlightened and broadminded statesman.

CHAPTER IX

Law's designs against England's political and industrial position—Earl of Stair's correspondence with Mr. Secretary Craggs—Stair accused by Law of threatening the safety of the Bank—Stair's recall intimated—Lord Stanhope sent to conciliate Law—Threatened rupture between England and France over question of evacuation of Gibraltar—Stair endeavours to justify his hostile attitude towards Law—His apprehensions as to Law's purpose in acquiring South Sea stock—The humiliating nature of Stair's dismissal.

CHAPTER IX

The year 1720 was a momentous one in the history of the Mississippi Scheme. Its commencement was full of promise from many points of view. It witnessed the realisation of Law's ambition to gather into his hands the reins of government in practically every department of the administration. It witnessed also the zenith of prosperity for all those gigantic schemes and undertakings which were to make France the great centre of trade and finance for the world. But the promise for the future which these circumstances seemed to contain was only of few months' duration. Yet these few months saw Law the most striking and commanding figure of his time throughout Europe. We have already seen the position to which he had attained in the internal affairs of France itself; how the government of that country was practically under his control; and how by sheer energy and force of character he had extended his influence over every class of society. His fame however reached far beyond the confines of France. He was regarded as an international force by other nations. Not only was his system copied by other countries, but he was bent on following a line of foreign policy for France which threatened the political and industrial prospects of these countries, and caused them great alarm, temporary no doubt, probably foolish, but real while it lasted.

Law's designs were chiefly directed against the power

of England. The English government recognised this, and considered Law a person to be conciliated. Their attitude towards him was peculiarly weak, and led to the recall of the minister at the French court, the Earl of Stair. That minister on his arrival in Paris in 1715 had called upon Law, not only as a friend, but because he adjudged him even then as a man of great importance. Their friendship however was of short duration. It rapidly degenerated into merely formal intercourse, and then into active hostility. The latter stage was reached in 1719, when we find Lord Stair intriguing against Law in his attempt to displace Dubois, foreign minister of France, by Torcy, who would have been a more pliable instrument for the carrying out of his designs. Lord Stair's letters to Mr. Secretary Craggs at this time are full of interest, and show the nature of the hostility between himself and Law, and the progress of their quarrel. On August the 30th, 1719, he writes—"In a long conversation I had with the Abbé (Dubois) to-night, he seems apprehensive that Torcy gains ground, and that there may be a close connection betwixt Law and Torcy, with views to turn the Abbé out. I am afraid this apprehension of the Abbé is not without ground; but, however that may be, I am persuaded we shall quickly see this court take airs which will not be easy to bear; and I am not a little apprehensive that we shall very quickly see them come into measures that we shall have no reason to like. If this should be true, we must not, in my poor opinion, seem to take any notice of it; but at the same time, it will behove us to exert ourselves to find out ways, without loss of time, to get rid of the pressure of the public debts." A few days later Lord Stair had apparently concluded that he was powerless to stem the advance of Law's influence, and writes accordingly—"Supposing I had talents, and that I were fitter to serve you at this court than another; you will be obliged to change your minister. You may depend on it, this court, with their fortune, will change their measures (i.e., their foreign policy); and they will desire to have a man here that they may be either able to gain or impose upon. You must henceforth look upon Law as the first minister, whose daily discourse is, that he will raise France to a greater height than ever she was, upon the ruin of England and Holland. You may easily imagine I shall not be a minister for his purpose. He is very much displeased with me already, because I did not flatter his vanity by putting in Mississippi. I did not think it became the King's Ambassador to give countenance to such a thing, or an example to others to withdraw their effects from England, to put them into the stocks here; which would have been readily followed by many. I have been in the wrong to myself, to the value of thirty or forty thousand pounds, which I might very easily have gained if I had put myself, as others did, into Mr. Law's hands; but I thought it was my duty, considering my position, not to do so.

The Abbé told me, that if some people prevailed, measures would be changed; that Torcy of late took the ascendant very much; and that the Regent discovered a great partiality towards him; and that, if it continued a little longer, he, the Abbé, would lay down. I am sure Law is in this thing, for he will be for removing everything that does not absolutely depend on him, and that can, in any manner, stand in his way to hinder him to be first minister. Law's heart has been set upon that from the beginning; and we stand too directly in the way of his ambitious views, for France to imagine that a good understanding can subsist long between the nations, if he comes to govern absolutely."

On the 9th of September, Lord Stair returns to the question of the displacement of Dubois, and seeks to impress the government with what he conceives to be the gravity of the situation.—"I told you, in my former letter, what the Abbé Dubois said to me upon the subject of Torcy's taking the

ascendant over him in the Regent's favour, and of the close
connection he, the Abbé, apprehended was between Torcy and
Law. He has since confirmed the same thing to me in several
conversations; and seemed to be in very great concern, and to
have thoughts of laying down, which I advised him not to do.
The Abbé likewise told me that there were many things which
were hid from him; and that he apprehended there was some
change of measures.

I come now to take notice of another thing to you, which in
my opinion is very much to be minded; and that is the spirit,
behaviour and discourse of the man whom, from henceforth,
you must look upon as the first minister, and that is Mr. Law.
He, in all his discourse, pretends that he will set France higher
than ever she was before, and put her in a condition to give
the law to all Europe; that he can ruin the trade and credit
of England and Holland whenever he pleases; that he can
break our Bank whenever he has a mind, and our East India
Company. He said publicly the other day at his own table,
when Lord Londonderry was present, that there was but one
great kingdom in Europe, and one great town; and that was
France and Paris. He told Pitt that he would bring down our
East India stock, and entered into articles with him to sell him
at twelve months hence a hundred thousand pounds of stock at
eleven percent, under the present current price.

You may imagine what we have to apprehend from a man of
this temper, who makes no scruple to declare such views, and
who will have all the power and all the credit at his court."

Later in the same month he says, "I hope our good friends
in the North will make our affairs in Parliament easy. We must
in that case exert ourselves to do something decisive towards
the payment of the public debts, if we do not intend to submit
ourselves to the condition in which Mr. Law pretends to put
all Europe. He says, *il rendra la France si grande que toutes les*

nations de l'Europe, enverront des Ambassadeurs à Paris, et le roy
n' enverra que des couriers."

From opposition on the ground of policy alone to personal differences was an easy stage. Law, conscious of his own power, had been hitherto somewhat indifferent to the efforts of Lord Stair to weaken his direction of the foreign policy of France. A rumour, however, which gained circulation towards the end of the year determined him to rid the French court of a man who he thought was moved not less by personal enmity than by the interests of the country he represented. Two circumstances had happened of an alarming nature which threatened the safety of the Bank and the value of Mississippi stock. A run had been made upon the Bank, and an attack upon the market had been organised with a view to depreciating the price of shares. These disturbing events had been attributed to Lord Stair, and Law at once informed the Regent to whom the matter was of great concern. Lord Stair was innocent of the charge, and naturally sought an interview with the Regent in order to disabuse his mind. The result was satisfactory so far as the assurances of the Regent went, but displayed the latter's duplicity since he was throughout unquestionably on the side of Law. Stair's letter descriptive of the interview was dated the 11th of December.—"Several days ago I was informed on very good authority, that Mr. Law told the Duke of Orleans that it was I who had latterly been the cause of the attack on the Bank. I thereupon resolved to clear myself with him, and I turned the conversation in such a way that he mentioned he had been told that I had been the cause of the attack. I said to him, 'My Lord, I understand that Mr. Law has had a talk with you, and I am very pleased to have the opportunity of proving to you that he is absolutely false in all his statements. It is true that the subjects of the King, my master, have considerable wealth in this country, which it would have been very easy for me to

have used to the prejudice of the Bank. But if it is true that
neither I nor any other subject of the King had taken *billets*
in order to have them changed at the Bank; if we have not
placed shares on the market in order to depreciate them; if it is
true that I have had no communication with those who have
run on the Bank, you ought to be convinced that Mr. Law's
talk is not only false but is the most atrocious calumny and the
most unworthy; a calumny which does not tend only to deceive
you on my account, a trustworthy servant at all times, through
gratitude and through affection; but which tends to embroil
you with my master, the King, who is your best friend and ally;
for I know that Mr. Law stated at the same time that what I did
in this respect I did by order of my court.

Now, if Mr. Law cannot prove to you that one of these
three points is true, since I boldly submit to you that all three
are false, he ought to be considered by you as a calumniator
who desires to deceive in things of great importance. But it
is not merely of recent date that I know the good intentions
of Mr. Law for his country, and the designs he has to set the
King at variance with you. It is only eight days since Mr. Law
publicly threatened, in presence of several subjects of the King,
my master, to write a book for the purpose of convincing the
world that Great Britain could not possibly pay her debts. Such
are the ordinary and public discourses of Mr. Law. You can
judge what effect that can produce when a man who pretends
to be your first minister delivers such discourses. I have known
it for a long time, but I have refrained from saying anything
to you because I was persuaded that Great Britain would not
think the same; and because I regarded these discourses as the
effects of the foolish vanity and inebriation of Mr. Law whose
head I have noticed for some time, has been turned.' I then told
the Duke of Orleans many discourses of a similar nature. The
Duke listened with surprise. At last he said to me, 'My Lord,

they are truly the discourses of a fool.' I replied, 'I say nothing to you that I would not say in Mr. Law's presence, and that I could not prove; you can now judge if it would have been astonishing if I had really acted in the way Mr. Law led you to believe I had done, but I am guided by the respect I have always had for your interests.' The Duke of Orleans told me finally that he was quite satisfied with what I had just told him; that he had always looked on me as his friend, and that he had difficulty in believing that I wished to prejudice his operations. That is substantially all that passed between the Duke and myself on the subject of Mr. Law. You can make the necessary reflections. There is no need of comment."

Stair's following letter communicates an apparent determination of the Regent to exclude Law from any influence on the relations of France with England, but also indicates his hesitation to place too much reliance upon the Regent's assurances. "The Regent," he writes, "so strongly perceived the dangers into which Law would precipitate him, that some days ago he repeatedly spoke very strongly to me of the vanity, presumption, and insolence of this man. He said he knew Law to be a man whose head had been turned by excessive vanity and ambition; that nothing could satisfy him except to be absolute master; that he had so great conceit of his own abilities and so great contempt for the talents of other men that he was impracticable with every one; that he had tried to make him work with the cleverest men in France, and that he could not agree with them for two consecutive days, always being impatient at the slightest obstacle or contradiction. He told me that he had rated Law soundly for his insolent discourses which alarmed everyone in such a way that he had reason to believe that Law would contain himself; but that he saw clearly no bridle could hold him. 'But,' said the Regent, 'believe me, I shall arrange matters so that there will be no risk of Law embroiling me with the King nor separating me from my allies. He is necessary to me in my financial affairs, but he will not be listened to in political matters, and I shall be on my guard against his mischievous designs.' I should like to believe that the Regent said what he thinks, and that he really thought it at the moment he spoke to me; but, with all that, a great treasurer, such as Law, is first minister wherever he chances to be in office; and if Law's system is established we are equally lost sooner or later. Further, believe me, we ought to be aware of this nation; we can never, with safety, count on their friendship, inasmuch as you could be a dangerous enemy to them, and can bring home to them the great injury we could cause them if they disagreed with us. On this account their friendship will be assured; but we shall miscalculate every time we depend on them in time of need. You will have received a messenger from the Abbé Dubois, who would inform you that I told him last Thursday that I would ask to be recalled. It is not from pique; but I see by the course things are taking that I shall no longer be able to render any service to the King at this court."

In the middle of January, 1720, Lord Stanhope intimated the recall of Lord Stair to the French minister, and a few days afterwards it was known throughout Paris. The manner of his recall was by no means courteous, but Lord Stair received the news with apparently unruffled temper, and expressed no regret in dimitting office since he recognised the difficulty and the delicacy of the position in which he had placed himself. Notwithstanding, however, the manner of his discharge—a discharge which was virtually a disgrace—he declared that it would not alter his unchangeable devotion to the service of his King and country. So serious a view did the English government take of the probable consequences of Stair's efforts to circumvent Law that they deemed it necessary to send Lord Stanhope himself to Paris in order to conciliate Law and to disclaim any animosity on the part of England towards him. Such a step showed at once a callous indifference to the feelings of Lord Stair, and greatly gratified Law, who seemingly occupied the proud position of being able to bring England to the humiliating necessity of asking his pardon for the hostility to him of her minister. Stanhope also promised to give Law's son a regiment, and to secure that a writ of summons should be issued calling Lord Banbury, his brother-in-law, to the House of Lords, a question as to his title having arisen which had hitherto denied him this privilege. Lord Stair refers to this step by his government in a letter dated the 14th of February, 1720. "As to Lord Stanhope, I have ever had a very great value and esteem for him; and I have upon all occasions endeavoured to give him the sincerest proofs of my friendship and faithful attachment to him; and I dare say it, with great truth, that I have not given him the least reason to complain of me personally. I am sorry if I have not been able to deserve his esteem, but I am sure I have deserved his friendship, at least his good-will. What has happened lately, I own to you, has piqued me very much, especially the manner of doing it; but I reckon that has proceeded from his views as a minister, in which I think he has been very much mistaken. I shall readily agree with you that if his lordship has gained Mr. Law, and made him lay aside his ill-will and ill-designs against his country, he did very right to make all sorts of advances to him, to give his son a regiment, to engage to bring Lord Banbury into the House of Lords, to sacrifice the King's ambassador to him. If I had thought Mr. Law to be gained, I should very readily have advised to do all these very things and a great deal more. But if his lordship has not gained Mr. Law I am afraid we shall not find our account in Lord Stanhope's supporting, when he is ready to fall, in making him first minister, and in destroying the personal credit I had with the Regent, and recalling me from this court, when my

long stay should have enabled me to be better able to judge
of their designs and of their ways of working than a stranger
of greater capacity could probably be. A little time will show
who has judged right. I do most heartily wish, for the good
of my country, that I may be found to have framed a wrong
judgment; but I own to you I have seen nothing yet to make
me change my opinion, but on the contrary, new things every
day do confirm me that Mr. Law's designs and the views of
this court are just what I represented them to be. You do me
great wrong if you say that I advised to break with the Regent
if he did not agree to part with Mr. Law. You will find no such
thing in any of my letters. You will find then, that I thought
it was useful to endeavour to shake Mr. Law's credit with his
master, to make his master jealous of Mr. Law's ambition, and
apprehensive of the dangers his presumption might lead him
into; and that I thought it was fit to stand in his way, as much
as it was possible, to hinder him to gain an absolute power over
the Regent's mind, and to obstruct his becoming first minister.
I thought it was fit to make Mr. Law lose his temper and to
make him act in passion and rage. I had not succeeded in all
these views when Lord Stanhope arrived and thought fit to
demolish me and all my works at once. As to Mr. Law, I have
no ill-will to him, but as I take him to be a dangerous enemy
to my country, I am afraid time will but too plainly show that
I have judged right in this matter. As to my revocation, if it was
possible I should have a mind to stay in this country, you have
made it impracticable. You have taken all effectual ways that
could be thought of to destroy the personal credit I had with
the Regent. You have made it plain to him that I have no credit
with the King, that is to say with his ministers. Lord Stanhope
has declared to Mr. Law that I shall be recalled, so that is
no longer a question. You are under the necessity of sending
another minister to this court."

A new element of concern for Lord Stair now introduced itself, and bulked largely in his subsequent correspondence up to the time of his departure from Paris. The occupation of Gibraltar by Britain was a sore point with France and Spain, and many efforts were made at various times to obtain her dislodgment. Lord Stanhope's visit to Paris at this time was taken advantage of by the Regent and Dubois for the purpose of negotiating its evacuation if possible, and, according to Stair, he had given some hope of this being brought about. On the faith of this, the Regent had apparently assured the King of Spain that Gibraltar would be given up, and felt that his honour was now involved in this hope being realised. It was soon evident however that the English government had no intention at any time of entertaining proposals for its evacuation, and alarm was felt that a rupture might take place. Law, we are informed by Stair, was anxious to declare war, and was confident that the resources of France, owing to the operation of his system, were sufficient to result in a successful issue. He became very bitter in his conversation about England, and spoke with a degree of insolence, revolting even to the French. One evening he invited to dinner Lord Bolingbroke, and so fierce was his denunciation of the English that the latter vowed he would never again set foot in Law's house. On the same occasion one of Stair's friends had said to Law, "Sir, what is this rumour which runs through Paris about us going to have war? I am persuaded that you have nothing to do with it. A man who thinks of making a flourishing state by commerce, and by the establishments which require peace, does not think of war." Law replied coldly to him, "Sir, I do not wish war, but I do not fear it."

Lord Stair's conclusions were undoubtedly biased by the deep feelings of resentment he naturally fostered towards the man who had accomplished his downfall, and he was too ready to make use of any rumour which in any degree gave colour to the character of the designs he attributed to Law. There is no substantial evidence that Law really went so far as Stair would have us believe, and was using every means in his power to induce the Regent to make the question of Gibraltar an occasion for hostilities. It is impossible to say more than that Law was merely an interested spectator, but not an active participant during the progress of the affair. As first minister, he would be under the necessity of guarding his opinions when expressed upon the subject, but there is no reason to believe that he meant more than he said when he stated he did not wish war, but did not fear it. Yet Stair sees underlying this remark the insolence of Law with which he has been endeavouring to impress the government at home, and points out that if this be his attitude when his system is likely to fall to pieces, what would it be if his system yet proved a success.

Notwithstanding Stair's efforts, however, the English government were not inclined to adopt his views as to Law's designs, and indicated that he had simply allowed himself to be carried away by pique and bad temper. Stair could not of course allow an accusation such as this to pass unchallenged and replied, "God knows, that I was only actuated by feelings of zeal and of attachment towards my King and to my country. I have spoken truly, as a clear-headed man, whilst you have treated me as a dreamer; although I can say, without conceit, that you have reason to trust me and to distrust those to whom you have given trust. I do not speak of Lord Stanhope. I know him to be an honest man, and a faithful servant of the King. I respect him and honour him; and although I have had cause to complain of him, I have no resentment against him. He believed he was serving the State in humiliating me. He was deceived. Any man can be deceived. I'll be bound for it, if you had left it to me, Law would have been lost at the present moment, and the understanding between the King and the Duke of Orleans would have been closer than ever. At the present time it is necessary to think as soon as possible about sending another minister to this court. For God's sake, send an honest man here before everything; and a clever man if you can find him."

Stair seems to have created an impression in the mind of his government that he wished the King to demand from the Regent a promise that he would depose Law from office at the risk of going to war; and early in March, Mr. Secretary Craggs wrote that the King would not entertain such a proposal. Stair had not, however, reduced the matter to such an issue, and on the 12th of March stated clearly the position he had taken up. "I must beg pardon," he wrote, "to say two things, first that I never did put things upon that issue, and in the next place, that there was no need of putting things upon that issue. You will find in my letters that I represented to the Duke of Orleans that Law, by his vanity and presumption, was leading him into great dangers and inconveniences, both at home and abroad; that Law, by going too fast, and by taking arbitrary measures, was in a way to ruin his Royal Highness's credit with the nation, and to overturn the whole system of the finances; and that, at the same time, Law was, by his discourse and conduct, doing everything that lay in his power to destroy the good understanding between the King and the Regent, and between the Regent and the rest of his allies, and I bade the Regent beware how he trusted the reins of his chariot to that Phaeton Law, because he would overturn it. The answer the Regent made me to these representations was, that he knew that vanity and ambition had turned his head; but that he, the Regent, would take care to keep a hand over him, and to contain him within bounds in the management of the finances; that he should have nothing to say in public affairs; that, if he pretended to meddle, the Regent would not listen to him; and that I might be well assured that it should not be in his power to create an ill understanding between him and the King.

I believe nobody can fairly say that there is anything in my representations which imported that the King would quarrel with the Regent if he did not lay Law aside. Nor can they say that there is anything in the Regent's answer which imports that he took what I said in that sense. On this foot things stood. I spoke very freely to the Regent what I had to say on the subject of Mr. Law, and His Royal Highness received what I said in a very friendly manner.

When Lord Stanhope arrived, he thought fit to acknowledge Mr. Law as first minister, and to consider him as a much greater man than ever Cardinal Richelieu or Cardinal Mazarin had been; to tell the Regent that the King was very well satisfied with Mr. Law, and did not in any manner complain of him; that what I had said was entirely out of my own head, and without, and even contrary to orders; and that for so doing I should be recalled. Since that time Mr. Law has acted as First Minister, and I have had no intercourse with the Regent but in formal audiences, to deliver such messages as I received from Court, and to receive short and formal answers.

In what manner Mr. Law has acted as First Minister, I may save you the trouble of telling you. You have seen it and felt it.

For me; there was nothing left for me to do, but to desire to be recalled, unless I could have prevailed with myself to have acted the part of a fool, or of a knave, or of both. What I have said above, I believe, is sufficient to prove that things were not brought to that extremity that there was a necessity to declare war against France, or to make humble submission to Mr. Law.

What has happened of late may convince you, I am sure it will the world, that I knew Mr. Law and this court better than other people do. Neither vanity or resentment prompts me to say this.

As to the charge you bring against me, that I have exclaimed against the minister personally, and against these measures, it does not lie against me. I have behaved myself with great modesty and moderation on this side. I have never spoken of Lord Stanhope but with respect and esteem. I have writ upon that subject to yourself with great freedom, and to no other man living, my uncle Sir David excepted, to whom I endeavoured to clear myself of the heavy charge you brought against me. I shall not compare my behaviour with that of other people's. I know how I have been represented to my master and my country. I propose no other revenge to myself than to show by my conduct that they have been unjust to me, and that I deserved fairer usage.

If the charge you mention is laid against our ministry, *viz.*, 'That Law is for setting up the Pretender, and they are setting up Mr. Law; that the Regent will play us false; and that I have been ill-treated for penetrating these designs; that we are in the hands of France and dare not own it; that he understands himself with Spain, and that we shall be the dupes of this alliance, and of this war.' If this charge is laid against the Ministers, it shall not be laid against them by my words. I shall content myself to shew my conduct, that no part of that charge lies against me.

Believe me, my dear Craggs, I have no design to enter into any cabals, nor to make any broils in the state. If I endeavour to show you are wrong, it is with a design that you may get into the right way again as soon as possible, that you may not continue to deceive yourselves. Ask and take the assistance of people who love the King and his government. You shall always be sure of my little help to support this ministry. I am not for changes; nor can I be influenced by private resentment, which, I declare to you upon my honour, I am ready to forget, as if I never had any reason to complain. My dear Craggs, take my word for it, Mr. Law's plan is formed to destroy the King and

his government and our nation; and he will certainly bring his
Master into it; nor is there any other way to divert him from
that design but my showing his Master that it is dangerous
for him to attack us. There is nothing but an appearance of
strength and firmness on our side, or the miscarriage of Law's
system on this side, can save us from a war with France. No
personal credit that anybody may flatter themselves they have
with the Duke of Orleans, will signify anything to divert it.
Your letter about Gibraltar was very well writ, and it was very
right to write it; but I will give you my word for it, it will have
no manner of weight here if Law's system takes place. If they
can bully the Ministry, or buy a party in England, we must part
with Gibraltar; and when we have parted with it we shall be
every way as little secure of peace as we are at present; and upon
many accounts less able to support a war."

Fresh apprehension seems to have been aroused in Stair's
mind as to Law's apparently deep designs for the accomplishment
of some great injury to English interests by the fact that Law
about this time had purchased large quantities of South Sea
stock. He communicated his apprehension to Craggs, who was
not disposed to lay great stress upon the circumstance. This
seems to have somewhat allayed his fears, and he accordingly
wrote on the 30th of April:

"I am glad you do not apprehend that Mr. Law is in a
condition to do us any great hurt by what he gets by the rise of
our South Sea Stock. Though I know that Law will brag, yet
I own to you I did apprehend that he had gained considerably
and that he might be able to do us a good deal of mischief by
withdrawing a very great sum himself, and by tempting other
foreigners to follow his example. I suppose you know the great
sums Mr. Law pretends to have in our stocks were bought in
Holland.

It seems to me to be a very dangerous thing in such a country as ours, where things are so very uncertain and fluctuating, to have foreigners masters of such vast sums of money, as they must needs have at present, by the rise of our stocks. This is a terrible handle to hurt us by, in the hands of such a man as Law. I wish our monied men may be attentive enough to the security of the nation in this point; and that they may not let themselves be blinded by the flattering appearances of present gains.

I am very glad to see you think so sanguinely as to the payment of our national debts. It will be very important to give the world such impressions of our situation. By several letters I have seen from very understanding men in Holland, I should be afraid that such impressions might prevail there and at Geneva, which would be very hurtful to us, for both the Dutch and the Geneve have very great sums in our stocks.

I am afraid we have not money enough, either in coin or in paper, to move so vast a mass as our South Sea Company now comes to be. The national bank would have been a very great help. I must own I apprehend that if that matter is not settled at this time, you will meet with great opposition at any other time by the South Sea Company, which, from this time forward, we are to look upon as a very powerful body.

I am afraid our people in England think too neglectfully of Mr. Law's schemes. I own to you, that, as this kingdom is disposed, there is a great odds to be laid that it will miscarry; but it is not impossible, far from it, that it may hold long enough to do us a good deal of mischief. Another thing I dare be bold to say—it cannot succeed without undoing us; and if Mr. Law can compass our ruin, I think he is in a fair way to carry through his project in France. I know Mr. Law himself thinks so too, and that being the case we may be very sure he will do us all the mischief in his power. You cannot think that power is small, considering the absolute authority he has acquired over the Regent. That being so I am sure you will agree with me that we cannot be too attentive to discover, prevent, and defeat the designs he may form against us. His designs are no trifling ones; they strike at the root. As to the behaviour of this court towards ours, it will depend entirely upon what happens in Sicily, and upon the King of Spain's disposition towards the Regent, which is naturally bad, and which, I have reason to think will not be made better by the advice he receives from France. As to our friend the new Archbishop of Cambray, (the Abbé Dubois) he will do Law all the hurt he can, because he is firmly persuaded that Law is determined to turn him out. The truth of the matter is that Law does hate and despise him exceedingly, and it is no less true, that the Abbé has but very little credit at present with his master, though his master affects to say the contrary. The Abbé, with all the desire he has to flatter himself, sees through the disguise."

The closing letter of this correspondence shows how humiliating was the dismissal of Lord Stair,—humiliating even to the extent of his being denied the usual privilege of seeing his sovereign on his return and how complete was the triumph of Law over his former friend:

"I see plainly I shall not be able to see the King of England. It is a great while ago since Mr. Law told his friends here, that I should not be allowed to have the honour of seeing the King. It is pretty hard to digest I own, if, after serving the King very faithfully, very zealously, and with some success, I should have the mortification not so much as to have my master's good countenance. However that happens to be, I am very glad His Majesty's affairs go so very well, and that there is so good an understanding amongst them that serve him.

I shall be able to tell a good many curious particulars concerning the state of affairs here, which are not so very proper to be put into a letter. Mr. Law still brags that he will make our stocks humble, by withdrawing the French effects. He seems more bent than ever to do us mischief, believing it the only way he has left to save himself and his system. How far he may be able to draw his master into his notions, God knows. His master professes the best intentions imaginable. In the meantime they go on with the new levies with all the application imaginable; and I am assured they are giving out commissions for levying some more German regiments in Alsace. All over France they talk of a war with Britain, and the Jacobites are in greater numbers at Paris, and more insolent. They talk of great changes at this court; and that the Archbishop of Cambray is to be sent to his diocese. Law's friends give out that he has more credit than ever at the Palace Royal. That may be; but I dare swear he has lost a great part of his master's good opinion, though, at the same time, he is very unwilling to renounce the fine views Law had given him. I think we have nothing to fear from France at present but by surprise; but, in my opinion, it will behove us to be very attentive against something of that kind. It is plain the Jacobites have their heads filled with some such notion.

As soon as Sir Robert arrives, I shall certainly set out and leave some friends to take the best care thay can to my effects."

Thus was brought to a close an embassy which offered at its outset so bright promises, but which ended in virtual disgrace. It is very questionable if any other result could have been possible. Lord Stair possessed all the necessary qualifications for a successful ambassador, and his failure can hardly be said to have been due to want either of ability or of tact. Rather was it due to the integrity of his motives and to the high estimate he had of his office. Had he yielded to the temptation which Law set before him to enrich himself by speculation in Mississippi stock, his difference with him might never have originated, and his mission might have had a happy ending. But it is futile to speculate on probable consequences had events been other than they really were. On the other hand it is a tribute to Lord

Stair's foresight that he always predicted the downfall of Law's schemes, and this he did even when they were at the height of their prosperity and gave every indication of probable success.

CHAPTER X

The beginning of Law's difficulties—The Bank's reserve of specie begin to be depleted—Law attempts a remedy by altering the standard of the coinage, and restricting the currency of specie—Temporary success of remedy—Domiciliary visits resorted to for detection of hoarded specie—Bank and Company United—Discharge of National Debt—Use of the Rue Quincampoix prohibited as a stock market—The assassination of a stock-jobber by the Comte de Horn, and the latter's execution.

CHAPTER X

Events now very rapidly developed in the history of the Bank and of the West India Company. Law's accession to power marked the beginning of his difficulties—difficulties which taxed his judgment to the utmost and forced him into the employment of expedients which he himself foresaw could not permanently ward off injury to his schemes. He thought, however, they might serve their purpose until his schemes assumed a less fluid condition, and that their establishment in good working order would render them proof against attack from such outside forces as might array themselves against him.

The first indications of danger were becoming apparent in December, and by the following month had assumed an alarming aspect. Shares had been selling at the very high price of 10,000 livres each, but by concerted action amongst several large holders and speculators that price was gradually forced up until it reached the unprecedented figure of 20,000 livres. This was now their opportunity. Artificial inflation could not be carried to greater lengths, and accordingly a process of extensive unloading commenced. These speculators, however, suspicious of the stability of the new system, were not satisfied with holding notes, the value of which might depreciate at any moment, and immediately presented them at the Bank for their equivalent in specie. Law perceived that such a process if allowed to run unchecked would soon deplete the Bank of all its available resources. Refusal to exchange would be suicidal, and if public confidence could not be maintained without recourse to artificial means, the currency of the notes would require to be forced directly or indirectly.

One of the chief offenders was the Prince de Conti, a near relative of the Regent. This nobleman had amassed great wealth through engaging in speculation under Law's guidance, but had alienated the latter by his insatiable appetite for still greater fortune. Unable again to enlist the services of Law in his interests, he evinced towards him that bitterest form of ingratitude, the ingratitude of the man who is favoured to him who does the favour. He attacked Law in his most sensitive part by realising great quantities of stock, and converting the notes he received in payment into money at the Bank, an operation which required the aid of three wagons. Many speculators who had preferred specie to paper transmitted their money abroad for safe investment, and in the course of a few weeks several hundred millions of livres were sent out of the country. A few also hoarded their wealth in secret places until the time would come when they could without fear employ it openly.

The first step taken by Law with a view to placing a check upon this continuous drain on the reserves of the Bank was the issue of a decree on the 28th of January, depreciating the coinage by raising the price of the silver marc to 54 livres. At the same time the interest of money was reduced from four to two percent. Many people refused to bring their specie to the Bank for recoinage, and then commenced that system of domiciliary visits which under subsequent decrees worked with so much tyranny and for a time absolutely destroyed not only public but also domestic confidence.

The result of the decree was not so satisfactory as had been anticipated, and in quick succession other decrees were issued introducing alterations in the standard of the coinage. The purpose of this was to discredit specie as far as possible as a medium of exchange, and by giving the note the appearance of fixity in value to raise its credit for currency purposes. Payments in specie were only allowed to the extent of 300 livres in gold, and of ten livres of silver, sums respectively equivalent to £12 10s. and 8s. 4d. in our money. Public offices could only receive payments in banknotes, except where the amounts of these or the balances were less than the lowest denomination of the note. And then the employment of gold and silver for other than coinage purposes was strictly prohibited without the royal license. These measures, however, were still unequal to restoring public confidence in the paper of the Bank, although in addition to those already specified, decrees were published fixing the value of paper at five percent, and then at ten percent, above the corresponding nominal value of specie. Trade was now beginning to experience the bad effects of a restricted currency, and representations were strongly made to Law and to the Regent to restore the currency to its previous position. This of course Law was unable to do without facing the consequences of seeing the bulk of the specie withdrawn altogether not only from circulation but from the country. A financial and industrial crisis would have at once been precipitated. To meet the situation, Law resolved upon bold and extreme measures. On the pretext that there were 1,200,000,000 livres in specie lying idle in the hands of financiers and successful speculators, an edict of Council was published on the 27th of February, which ordered "that no person, of whatever estate or condition, not even any religious or ecclesiastical community, should keep more than 500 livres in coined money or ingots, under pain of confiscation of the excess, and of a fine of 10,000 livres." All payments exceeding 100 livres in amount were to be made without exception in paper, and the purchase of jewellery, plate

and precious stones was declared illegal if made for purposes
of investment. To provide against concealment of specie
informers were promised a reward of half the sums disclosed,
and all government officials were ordered to make search
wherever ordered by the directors of the Bank. This decree was
followed on the 5th of March by one which further debased
the currency by raising the price of the silver marc to 85 livres,
and on the 11th of March by a third, by which gold specie
was to be withdrawn from the currency from and after the 1st
of May following, and silver specie, except the smaller pieces
which were necessary for odd change, from and after the 1st of
August following.

These various decrees wrought a revolution in the fiscal
arrangements of the country. No one appreciated more fully their
danger than Law himself, but extraordinary circumstances such
as those with which he was forced demanded the employment
of extraordinary methods to counteract them. He was presented
with the alternative of certain collapse of his schemes if he did
not resort to arbitrary measures, or of a possible chance of
saving the situation if he could force the currency of paper by
withdrawing all the specie from circulation and holding it in the
hands of the Bank. Had he succeeded in doing this, confidence
in the notes of the Bank would undoubtedly have largely been
restored since that depends entirely upon the knowledge of the
public that behind them there are liquid reserves available for
conversion whenever required. It is questionable if any other
methods could have been devised than those followed by Law,
and in judging their character it is necessary to bear in mind
the ultimate object he had in view.

It was natural that these tyrannical steps should have had
the immediate effect of rousing a storm of opposition amongst
the public towards Law, and if we are to believe Lord Stair, they
also prejudiced him in the eyes of the Regent, to whom the

hostile attitude of the people was a matter of grave concern. On the day following the issue of the decree of the 11th of March, he wrote to Craggs, "The rage of the people is so violent, that, in the course of one month, he will be pulled to pieces; or his master will deliver him up to the rage of the people. You may depend upon it that he is mightily shaken in his master's good opinion, who, within these few days last past, has used him most cruelly to his face, and called him all the names that can be thought of, 'Knave and madman,' etc. He told him he did not know what hindered him to send him to the Bastille; and that there never was anyone sent thither deserved it half so well. To make matters better, Law's head is so heated that he does not sleep at nights, and he has formal fits of phrenzy. He gets out of bed almost every night and runs, stark staring mad, about the room making a terrible noise; sometimes singing and dancing, at other times swearing, staring and stamping, quite out of himself. Some nights ago his wife, who had come into the room upon the noise he made, was forced to ring the bell for people to come to her assistance. The officer of Law's guard was the first that came, who found Law in his shirt, who had set two chairs in the middle of the room and was dancing round them, quite out of his wits. This scene the officer of the guard told Le Blanc, from whom it came to me by a very sure conveyance. Le Blanc is in despair about the state of Law's health and discredit in which he stands with the Regent. At the same time, there is a most formidable party formed against him, and almost everyone who held their tongues out of fear, now take courage to speak to the Regent upon his character; so that they believe the Regent is only withheld by shame from sacrificing him to the resentment of the nation. Law, on the other hand, says, that if they will give him but a little time, he will set everything to rights; that he will raise the credit of the stocks; turn the course of the exchange; sink the stocks in England, and put everything in that country into such disorder that it shall plainly appear that he can do everything in that country he pleases. In order to that, he has prevailed with Croisset, Andé, and several other people, who had very great sums in our stocks, to withdraw their money and to remit the greater part of it back into France; with the rest, he proposes to turn the course of the exchange and to carry on his other designs. He proposes further, in order to alter the course of the exchange, to lower the value of the specie in France, till the crown is brought down by degrees to three livres; and this arret is to come out in a few days."

Law's object was to a large extent gained so far as it aimed at replenishing the reserves of coin at the Bank. During the month of March no less than 300,000,000 livres were deposited, a sum undoubtedly large but still short of being an adequate security against the enormous mass of paper afloat, which has been estimated at 2,600,000,000 livres. These deposits were at the same time maintained in full strength by the operation of the decree of the 27th of February, which relieved the Bank of the necessity of repaying at any time more than 500 livres in specie. Success however limited as it was, was only secured at considerable cost to Law's reputation. The domiciliary visits which were made use of for detecting hoarded coin created widespread and bitter resentment. A feeling of deep distrust, of insecurity, and of fear crept through the community. The reward for information was so great that sons betrayed their parents, brothers their sisters, servants their masters. Friend betrayed friend, and enemies had an effective instrument of revenge. "Never before had sovereign power been so violently exercised, never had it attacked in such a manner the temporal interests of the community. Therefore was it by a prodigy, rather than by any effort or act of the government, that these terribly new ordinances failed to produce the saddest and most complete revolutions; but there was not even talk of them; and although there were so many millions of people, either absolutely ruined or dying of hunger, and of the direst want, without means to procure their daily subsistence, nothing more than complaints and groans was heard."

Among those who were ruined in their fortunes at this time was one of the directors of the Bank itself. A domiciliary visit, prompted by one of his enemies, resulted in the discovery of 10,000 crowns, which were confiscated. For failure to declare his hoard and deposit it in the Bank he was fined 10,000 livres and lost his appointment. The brothers Paris were also among the sufferers. They were detected in the act of conveying 7,000,000 livres into Lorraine, and a visit to their residences brought into the coffers of the Bank an additional sum of like amount. These confiscations and many others of more or less substantial sums were published abroad in order to induce others to conform to the edict from fear, and in many cases the prospect of loss of fortune was regarded a less evil than possibility of discovery with all its attendant penalties. There is in fact every reason to believe that neither Law nor the Regent anticipated recourse to harsh measures in carrying out their decree. They relied upon the fear which would be created by its publication serving their purpose, and in order the better to accomplish it arranged with several well-known prominent men to allow themselves to become apparent victims. Thus were many of the courtiers and public officials intimidated into divesting themselves of their accumulated wealth, and into exchanging it for paper which was so soon to lose its value. The largest capture which was made was that of ex-Chancellor Pontchartrain whose cellars disgorged the enormous sum of 57,000 louis d'or or considerably over; £10,000,000. The deep dislike the Regent had for his own decree is also evinced by his conduct towards the President Lambert de Vernon, who had sought an interview for the purpose of informing against some one who was possessed of 500,000 livres in gold. On hearing his message, the Regent in horror enquired, "What d—d sort of a trade have you taken to?" The President replied, "Sir, I do nothing more than obey the law, and it is that which you indirectly treat with such an appellation. As for the rest, your Royal Highness need not be alarmed, and may do me more justice. It is myself I come to inform against, in the hope of being allowed to keep at least a part of this sum, which I prefer to all the bills of the Bank." As a result of his appeal, the President was allowed the reward of an informer and permitted to retain half his fortune.

Law himself was the victim of a somewhat amusing result of his own methods about this time. Some months before he negotiated with the President of Novion the purchase of his estates for 400,000 francs. The President required payment to be made in silver, and Law, who was anxious to impress everyone with the advantages to be gained by the use of paper alone, could not of course refuse, declaring that he preferred to be rid of a metal which was to him a burden on account of its bulk, and of the embarrassment it caused him. Unfortunately Law was compelled afterwards to re-transfer the estates to the President's son to whom the right of pre-emption had been reserved, and received back the price in notes which he was bound to accept according to his own decree. Nor could Law complain of the advantage that had been taken of him without depreciating the value of his own paper.

A measure of vastly greater importance and destined to lead to much graver consequences than even those already mentioned was the union of the Royal Bank and the Indian Company. A meeting was held on the 22nd of February at the Bank to which had been called the principal shareholders of the Company, the proposal being formally made and agreed to. Since the General Bank had been converted, in December,

1718, into a Royal institution, it had carried on its business for the benefit of the Royal revenues alone. The notes in circulation carried the guarantee of the King, a guarantee which was still to remain notwithstanding the amalgamation. For the ostensible purpose of preventing unlimited issue of additional notes it was provided that authority must in all cases be first obtained from the Council. Since the Council was in all its deliberations under the influence of the Regent, it will be seen later how worthless such a provision proved as an effective check to arbitrary fabrication of paper. During the period of the Bank's existence as a Royal establishment, it had carried on business with great success, its balance sheet showing on paper a profit 120,000,000 livres of profit. This profit it was also arranged should be transferred intact to the company for the benefit of its shareholders. The object which Law had in view in bringing about the union could only have been one of expediency. It contained no feature which promised permanent success to the undertaking, and showed a singular lack of foresight and real business capacity. Undoubtedly it gave encouragement to speculators, who were carried away by the apparent increase of stability given to the Company by the amalgamation. But even this was of short duration. It was impossible to conceal for long the illusory nature of the transaction, and it soon became clear that a false step had been taken inasmuch as the fortunes of the Bank were now altogether bound up with those of the Company.

Previously to the date of the incorporation of the Bank and the Company, the note issue in circulation amounted to about 600,000,000 livres. Within three months after that date, an additional 2,000,000,000 livres were fabricated and set afloat. The bulk of the fresh issues was utilised for the purpose of discharging the national debt, one of the great objects which Law had in view at the initiation of his financial schemes. The national creditors were now become creditors of the Company in respect of the notes they held; and the state had now nominally discharged her debts in full.

One of the difficulties created by the publication of the various decrees limiting the currency of coin was that of scarcity of notes of small denomination. On the 19th of April, accordingly, a decree was registered by which no less than 438,000,000 livres in notes of 10 to 1000 livres each were issued in order to facilitate the changing of notes of greater value and the carrying out of transactions of small amounts.

Although all these expedients failed in their object, the extent to which speculation was carried was very little affected. The time for suddenly made fortunes had now gone, but sufficient excitement remained to render the purchase and sale of shares an occupation attractive to thousands of speculators. The tendency of the market was distinctly downwards, but there were intervening fluctuations, which maintained the mania in almost all its former strength. The Rue Quincampoix was still crowded from morning till evening. So great were the crowds on many occasions that scenes of confusion were frequent and sometimes developed into scenes of violence. It formed a happy hunting ground for the lowest classes in the community. Robberies and even murders took place so often that special precautions had necessarily to be taken by those who carried money on their person. So dangerous had the street and its environs become that on the 22nd of March, the council published an edict prohibiting its use as a stock market, and requiring all houses and offices wherein share transactions had been hitherto usually negotiated to be closed in future for such business. No other locality was assigned to the speculators, and for two months they had no recognised place of meeting. The wisdom of this decree was dictated by an unhappy occurrence that took place on the morning of the day of its issue, in which was involved a young foreigner of noble family, Comte de Horn, son of Prince Philippe Emmanuel who had served in France at the sieges of Brizac and of Landau, and at the battles of Spire and of Ramillies. According to the account given of the incident by Duclos, it appears that the Count, who had been living a riotous life in Paris for some time and had contracted extensive debts, along with two companions, Laurent de Mille, and a sham knight named Lestang, plotted the assassination of a rich stock-jobber and the theft of his pocketbook in which he was known to carry large sums of money in paper. They resorted to the Rue Quincampoix, and under the pretext of negotiating the purchase of 100,000 crowns worth of shares, took the stock-jobber to a tavern in the Rue de Venise and stabbed him there. The unfortunate stock-jobber, in defending himself, made sufficient noise to attract the attention of a waiter, who, passing at the moment the door of the room, opened it. Seeing a man lying in a pool of blood, he immediately closed and locked the door and shouted murder.

The assassins, finding retreat closed against them, escaped through the window. Lestang, who had been keeping watch on the staircase, rushed off on hearing the shouts of the waiter to the lodging house in the Rue de Tournon, where the three of them boarded, took the most portable luggage and fled. Mille dashed through the crowds in the Rue Quincampoix, but followed by the people, was at last arrested at the markets. The Comte de Horn was seized on jumping from the window. Believing his two accomplices to have succeeded in saving themselves, he had enough presence of mind to say that he feared he himself would also have been murdered in trying to defend the stock-jobber. His ruse, however, proved valueless by the arrest of Mille, who, having been brought back to the tavern, confessed all. The Comte declared to no purpose he did not know Mille; and the Commissary of Police took him to prison. The crime being fully established, the trial did not last long, and on the 26th of March both were broken alive on the wheel in the Place du Grève. The Comte was apparently the author of the plot; for, while he was still breathing on the wheel, he demanded pardon for his accomplice, who was executed last.

Before the execution had been carried out, the strongest efforts had been made to influence the Regent to grant a pardon, or at least a commutation of the punishment. The crime was so atrocious that they did not insist on the first, but redoubled their solicitations for the latter. They represented that the execution by the wheel was so ignominious, that no daughter of the house of Horn could, until the third generation, enter any convent. The Regent rejected all prayers for pardon. They appealed to him on the ground that the culprit was allied to him, but he replied, "I shall partake of the shame. That ought to console the other relatives." He repeated the words of Corneille: "The shame is in the crime, not in the scaffold." The Regent was inclined however to commute the punishment, but Law and the Abbé Dubois impressed him with the necessity of preserving the public safety at a time when everyone carried his wealth about with him. They pointed out to him that the people would not be satisfied, and would consider themselves humiliated by a distinction of punishment for a crime so atrocious.

When his parents lost all hope of pardon from the Regent, the Prince de Robec Montmorency, and the Marechal d'Isenghen, found means of securing admission to the prison. They brought poison with them and exhorted him to take it in order to avoid the shame of the execution, but he refused. "You wretch," they declared, leaving him with indignation, "you are only worthy to die by the hands of the executioner."

CHAPTER XI

New measures prove ineffectual—New edict issued fixing price of shares and depreciating value of notes—Authorship of edict—People hostile to edict—Parliament refuses to register it, and a revocation is issued—Law deposed from office of Comptroller-General—d'Aguessau reinstated in his former office—New schemes for absorption of bank-notes— Widespread distress produced amongst community—Law's person in danger—Stock-jobbers establish themselves in the gardens of the Hotel de Soissons—Parliament exiled to Pontoise, and Bank closed for an indefinite period.

CHAPTER XI

The efforts of Law and of the Regent having as yet proved insufficient to rectify the balance between the notes in issue and the amount of specie in the country, the adoption of some final drastic measure was rendered imperative. A step was taken which has given rise to much controversy as to its authorship. On the 21st of May an edict of Council was issued, the provisions of which were designed to adjust the finances of the realm by one sweeping process, irrespective of the interests of individuals, and of a character so radical and effective as to exclude the possibility of the whim of the speculator from defeating its object. It not only covered the relations which were to obtain between the value of notes and specie, but also fixed the price of shares so that they should not disturb by their fluctuations the arrangements of the Bank. It enacted that on the date of publication of the decree banknotes of all denominations should suffer depreciation to the extent of 20 percent, of their value, and that on the first of each month, from the 1st of July to the 1st of December, further depreciation should take place to the extent of 500 livres on notes of the nominal value of 10,000 livres, and proportionately on the smaller notes. Shares were to undergo a similar diminution in value, starting from 8000 livres as at the 21st of May. On the 1st of December, therefore, all notes would have reached a discount of fifty percent, and shares would possess a fixed value of 5000 livres each. These regulations were to apply to all financial and industrial negotiations; but one exception was granted in the case of payment of Royal revenues, and purchase of state securities such as annuities, where until the 1st of December all notes would be received at their full face value. As a possible steadying influence in so disturbing and so confusing a change, the repeal of the edict prohibiting the currency of specie was to be withdrawn, and the standard value of the specie was again to be increased to a more normal ratio, the silver marc to stand at the value of 30 livres.

In the confusion of authorities it is extremely difficult to apportion the blame for the publication of the edict. On the one hand, it is stated that the enemies of Law were the instigators of it, and among them in particular Dubois and d'Argenson. These two ministers, desiring nothing more than the downfall of their rival, had suggested two courses by either of which the great disproportion between the notes and specie might be immediately accomplished. They pointed out to the Council that as the notes in issue were double in value the amount of specie, equality could be obtained by halving the value of the former or by doubling the value of the latter. Their suggestion possessed the element of simplicity and appealed very strongly to the other members, who, after serious discussion, and in spite of the remonstrations of Law as to its fatal consequences, determined upon dealing with the notes and leaving the specie at its present standard. On the other hand, it has been argued that the edict was really the work of Law and bears evident marks of his financial handiwork. Before the date of the decree, shares were at 10,000 livres in price, and the marc was valued at 85 livres. Consequently a share at that price represented almost 120 marcs. At the date of the last reduction, shares of 5000 livres would, with the increased ratio of value, return approximately

165 marcs to the holder, or a net gain of 45 marcs. The decree, therefore, which seemed to threaten the financial stability of the nation, would in reality have resulted not only in removing the difficulties due to the inflated issue of notes, but in benefiting materially all the shareholders of the company.

It is difficult to believe that Law on such a ground as this was the author of the decree. There is no contemporaneous evidence of its having been at any time advanced by himself or his friends in order to make the decree acceptable to the public, and it had the additional disadvantage of being unlikely to inspire any confidence. The immediate result of the decree, and not its probable result in the future, would be the determining factor in the attitude of the public towards it, and no one would understand this better than Law himself. It is more likely that Dubois and d'Argenson were accountable altogether for the decree, hoping thereby to secure his removal from office and to destroy the influence he had acquired in the government of the country. Law had made himself obnoxious to both. He had sought to undermine the authority of Dubois, and had deposed d'Argenson from the office of Comptroller-General. Their personal jealousy of the great foreigner was therefore sufficiently deep to take advantage of such an opportunity as they now had to avenge themselves.

The publication of the edict created universal consternation. The community were paralysed. The last shred of confidence in Law was utterly destroyed, and national bankruptcy was feared to be imminent. The attitude of the people was one of intense hostility, and threatened to break out at any moment into active riot. Multitudes flocked to the Bank, and the protection of the troops was required to maintain order. Nor was the fury of the mob appeased by the knowledge that the Duke of Bourbon, the Prince of Conti, and Marshall Villeroy, were strenuously opposed to the edict and demanded its withdrawal. Posters were exhibited all over the city calling upon the citizens to resist, even to the extent of using force. Hand-bills were distributed in thousands, foreboding a step of revolution. "This is to give you notice," they ran, "that a St. Bartholomew's day will be enacted again on Saturday or Sunday, if affairs do not alter. You are desired not to stir, you nor your servants. God preserve you from the flames. Give notice to your neighbours."

In the midst of this disorder the First President called Parliament together to consider the situation, and with prompt decision announced to the Regent their refusal to register the edict. The Regent, delighted to have this opportunity of reconciling himself with his Parliament, especially when the occasion allowed him to follow his own desires, received the parliamentary deputation with the greatest deference, and gave them assurance of his sympathy. He, accordingly, sent La Vrillière, one of the Secretaries of State, later on the same day to announce to the President his intention to withdraw the edict, and as far as possible restore the status quo which had been so ruthlessly disturbed. An edict was then published on the 27th of May, revoking that of the 22nd of May, by which shares and notes were allowed to remain at their previous value. Unfortunately, however, it was now impossible to restore public confidence. That was irretrievably lost. A blow had been struck at the system from which it never recovered. Its collapse may be dated from the ill-conceived edict of the 22nd of May, and its subsequent history is merely a record of measures of despair resorted to for the purpose of saving if possible some portion of the national credit.

Holders of banknotes now thought to avail themselves of the possibility of securing some portion at least of their paper changed into silver, but Law had foreseen the danger of allowing unlimited demands being made on the Bank, and suspended payment in order as he declared to enable him to investigate the circumstances of numerous frauds of which the Banks officials had been guilty. This proceeding, while demanded by the exigencies of the moment, merely added fuel to the fire, and the frenzied multitude only awaited the word of command from a leader to break out into open revolt. The notes in circulation were practically valueless for purpose of currency, and the greatest distress accordingly prevailed. The situation could not continue for many days in its present condition, and Law, in order to relieve the distress which was now universal, caused several thousand livres in specie to be sent to each of the commissaries in the city for exchange, but only to be given to those who satisfied the distributing authority that they required the specie for immediate wants. Thus again for a few days at least the inevitable liquidation was postponed.

The Regent was naturally much alarmed at the situation which had been created. He felt that his own position was largely bound up with that of Law, and that the hostile attitude of the community might also be directed against himself. He was urged by Dubois and other influential advisers to sacrifice Law, and thus secure the good favour of the community. The Regent, however, was unwilling to sever in a summary manner his intimacy with Law, but Law himself communicated his readiness to be discharged from office if the Regent thought it prudent in the interests of himself and of the nation. On the 29th of May, accordingly, the Regent through Le Blanc announced to Law that he no longer held the position of Comptroller-General of Finances, but that his services would still be retained as director of the Company and as a member of the Council. At the same time he informed Law that he intended to provide for his personal safety by giving him the protection of a detachment of Swiss Guards under the command of Benzualde. This precautionary measure was by no means superfluous. Law had been threatened by the mob and would have been stoned on one occasion while driving in his carriage had he not at the moment been near his own house and thus escaped. His family had also been subjected to similar treatment. The provision of a guard was therefore an act of kindly consideration for the deposed minister. On the day following his discharge, Law was taken to the Palais Royal by the Duc de la Force, but the Regent, in order to maintain the appearance of having disgraced him, refused to see him. The same evening, however, Law was sent for, and admitted by a secret door, and thus had the desired interview. Two days after these somewhat peculiar proceedings, Law and the Regent appeared together in public at the opera, the necessity for continuing the pretence of disgrace having evidently been regarded as needless.

Law, who acted at this critical period with great good sense, determined upon advising the Regent to reinstate d'Aguessau in the office of Chancellor from which he had been instrumental in removing him. With the assistance of Dubois, to whom Law had communicated his proposal and who strongly approved of its wisdom, as a prudent concession to public opinion, the appeal to the Regent was successful. Since his deposition, the ex-Chancellor had lived in retirement on his estate at Frênes. Thence Law himself, and the Chevalier de Conflans, an officer of the Regent's household, were despatched in order to convey the command of the King to resume his office. D'Aguessau at first refused to accept the honour, but after considerable pressure and on representations that the interests of the government lay with his acceptance, he agreed to receive the seals. D'Argenson was at the same time deprived of office, but retained all the honours and the position it had conferred upon him. Law's own successor was Pelletier des Forts, and associated with him as colleagues were d'Ormesson and Gaumont. These three formed a commission of finance, and to them was entrusted the responsibility of adjusting the finances of the kingdom.

As with Law, the supreme object of the new commission of finance was the reduction of the volume of banknotes in circulation and the establishment of the shares upon a more stable foundation in order to prevent the extravagant fluctuations to which they had hitherto been subjected. In their deliberations they were joined by five deputies of Parliament, a suggestion of the Regent who wished to impress the public with the idea that all the measures which might be taken to deal with the crisis had the approval of that body. The result of their deliberations was the creation of twenty-five million livres of annuities secured upon the revenues of Paris. These annuities, which bore interest at the rate of two and one-half percent, were purchasable in notes, which were received at their nominal value, and the notes thus utilised were to be burnt publicly at the Town Hall. At the same time it was determined to effect a wholesale reduction of the capital of the Company. The King was proprietor to the extent of 100,000 shares, and the Company itself held 300,000 shares which had been bought in during February and March at the rate of 9000 livres per share. These were now to be cancelled, and 200,000 new shares were to be issued in place of the 200,000 shares to which the capital was now reduced. The new shares were to be given to holders of the latter, share for share, with a liability of 3000 livres payable in notes or at the rate of two new shares for three old shares, and were to carry a fixed dividend of 360 livres per share. To induce the commercial community to make use of the facilities which the Bank were willing to afford, it was also arranged to open credit accounts for their benefit upon which they could operate to the extent of any deposits they might make in notes. It was hoped that these accounts would absorb at least 600,000,000 livres in notes, but so little advantage was taken of them that only about 250,000,000 livres were deposited.

These schemes, however, were only directed to absorption

of paper. They were valueless as means of relieving the distress of those who were in immediate need of money to satisfy the pressing wants of the moment. The price of food not only rapidly rose, but shop-keepers would only accept notes in payment at very high rates of discount, and in many cases refused to sell unless payment was made in specie. The distribution of silver by the commissaries had been of a very limited character, and merely served for the day upon which it was made. The probability of disturbances arising was strongly impressed upon the commission of finances unless provision was immediately made for extensive conversion of notes. It was accordingly arranged that the Bank should again be opened on the 10th of June for exchanging notes of 10 livres, and that on the 11th of June notes of 100 livres should also be exchanged for those of 10 livres. No more than one note of 10 livres was convertible into specie for each person, nor of 100 livres into small notes. These arrangements, designed with the best intentions, led unfortunately to a very alarming situation. The Bank was besieged by thousands of people during the few hours its doors were open, and a guard was stationed within the building to regulate the flow of the eager and excited multitude. Many were injured and crushed to death in the vast and unwieldy crowds, and the exasperating slowness of the process of exchange, by which only an insignificant portion of the crowd was satisfied each day, culminated not infrequently in attacks upon the soldiery who were thus under the necessity of charging them in order to prevent the possibility of the Bank being wrecked.

To relieve the Bank, recourse was had again to the employment of the district commissaries, whose offices were open on Wednesdays and Saturdays, but the same scenes were enacted there as at the bank itself. "The doors," says Buvat, "were only half open, so that the money seekers should only enter one by one, and none got in but the strongest. Most of them brought away nothing but sweat and fatigue instead of money, because the preferences that the commissaries gave to their friends had exhausted the funds, and they reserved a portion for themselves." This system of decentralising the distribution of specie was, however, of short duration, the Regent and his advisers fearing that the creation of numerous centres of disturbance might at any moment lead to widespread revolt.

Although the distribution of coin continued for several weeks, the needs of the community were still far from satisfied, and the crowds, instead of diminishing, grew larger each day. On the morning of the 17th of July, the crowd, who had commenced to gather at three o'clock, found their approach to the Bank protected by barricades so as to render the task of the guard less difficult in arranging the people in file. This measure of safety, however, only incited the people to violence, and determined them to destroy it. In the rush, by which it was hoped to carry away the barricades, a large number were seriously injured, and twelve were killed. Three of the bodies were forthwith carried to the Palais Royal, followed by a concourse of three or four thousand people thirsting for vengeance, and demanding the lives of Law and the Regent, both of whom were conceived to be the cause of the prevailing distress. The scene was impressive, and Paris seemed ready to rise in arms, but Le Blanc was equal to the situation and acted with promptness and tact. He ordered the guard at the Tuilleries to proceed at once to the Palais Royal. He himself reached the palace after the utmost difficulty, and with the greatest coolness informed the people who he was and that he had come to plead their case before the Regent. Addressing himself to those who had carried the bodies, he said, "My children, take these bodies, carry them to a church, and return to me immediately for payment." Surprised by the calmness of the Minister, they obeyed in spite of themselves, and a considerable portion of the crowd followed them, partly from curiosity and partly in hope of also participating in the reward. During their absence the guard arrived and dispersed the crowd without difficulty, the force of their demonstration having been destroyed by the removal of the bodies.

At ten o'clock on the same day Law drove to the Palais Royal to speak with the Regent. On the way he was recognised by the widow of one of those who had lost their lives earlier in the morning. At once the people surrounded his carriage and threatened to kill him. By preserving his usual coolness, however, he succeeded in reaching his destination without injury. The Regent, after the interview, would not allow Law to return home, and his carriage on making its appearance on the streets was again attacked and broken to pieces, the coachman barely escaping with his life. The news immediately spread through the city, and the First President who had left the chamber where Parliament was deliberating, hearing it rushed back to inform the members of what had happened. They rose to their feet and in excitement asked if Law too had been torn to pieces, but on the President replying that he was ignorant of all that had occurred, they adjourned the sitting in order that they might carry the news to their friends.

Since the Rue Quincampoix had been closed to the stock-jobbers no place had been allotted to them for carrying on their business. Transactions, however, were not less numerous now than they were before, and the events of the past few months did not destroy speculation in the shares of the Company. The extreme inconvenience of having no recognised place for meeting induced the Regent to consider the appeals made to him, and accordingly on the 2nd of June they were allowed to establish themselves in the Place Vendôme. In the beautiful open square, of which the Place Vendôme consisted, assembled daily the fashionable Parisians of the day. Tents were erected for the accommodation of stock-jobbers, and the host of gamesters, saloon-keepers and others who catered for the pleasures of the crowd. The noise however of the great multitude of people proved a source of much annoyance to the Chancellor whose court was held in the vicinity, and on his complaint being made to the Regent it was necessary to arrange for the removal again of the place of exchange. Thereupon the Prince de Carignan sold to Law his Hotel de Soissons at the price of 1,400,000 livres, reserving the gardens which extended to several acres. In these the Prince erected a large number of tents for the jobbers which he let at 500 livres per month, the revenue from all producing about 500,000 livres per annum. In order to secure that the tents should be utilised, the Prince succeeded in obtaining an edict prohibiting the conclusion of any transaction except in one of them, and this was done under pretext of providing against the loss and theft of pocket-books containing money. For three months the stock-exchange of Paris was held in the gardens of the Hotel de Soissons, and on the 29th of October, stock-jobbing was entirely prohibited, a penalty of 3000 livres being imposed upon any one found dealing in shares or notes.

A few days before the outbreak at the Palais Royal, the Regent on the advice of Law had drawn up an edict, conferring in perpetuity upon the Company the whole commercial rights and privileges of the kingdom on condition that it liquidated within a year 600,000,000 livres of banknotes by monthly instalments of 50,000,000 livres each. The operation of this edict would have had the effect of re-establishing the Company as a sound commercial undertaking and of removing from circulation the unsecured paper issue afloat, but this would only have been possible at the cost of ruining the whole community of private traders or at least of placing them at the mercy of the Company which might exercise their proposed privileges in an arbitrary and despotic manner. On the 16th of July the draft-edict was submitted for approval to the Council of the Regency, and this body agreed to send it for registration to the Parliament. The following day it was deliberated upon by that assembly, who refused to give it effect, 148 members going so far as to support a proposal that it should be returned to the Regent without acknowledgment or reply.

This unexpected check to the plans of the Regent and of Law produced the greatest consternation at court. They feared that the people would by the refusal infer the sympathy of Parliament with their position and might be encouraged to break out into revolt, although the refusal had not proceeded from motives so high and disinterested, but from feelings of opposition to Law and to every proposal he might suggest that would tend to rehabilitate confidence in the Company. The Regent, with Law, Dubois, and Le Blanc, then resolved in secret council upon the banishment of Parliament to Blois. The musketeers with four thousand soldiers were immediately put in readiness to accompany the refractory assembly on its journey on the following day. The musketeers were to surround the resident of the First President, and the soldiers were to take possession of the Grand Chamber early in the morning, and orders were to be conveyed to all the members that they were to betake themselves to their place of exile within forty-eight hours. At the last minute, however, d'Aguessau prevailed upon the Regent to send the members to Pontoise, a place within easy reach of Paris, instead of to Blois where it was hoped they would have sooner submitted to his wishes by reason of the many discomforts and inconveniences they would undergo owing to its greater distance from the capital. The members, accordingly, proceeded on the 21st of July to Pontoise in a body without demur, determined to maintain their authority and equally determined to enjoy the term of their exile. The change of place of exile and all the circumstances connected with it converted what was intended as a punishment into proceedings of a highly ridiculous character. In order to assist those who might require money for their journey, the Regent sent to the Attorney General 100,000 livres in silver and a similar amount in notes. The First President was allowed a considerable sum in addition for his own expenses and drew from the Regent no less than 500,000 livres in all. "He kept open table for the Parliament; all were every day at liberty to use it if they liked, so that there were always several tables all equally, delicately, and splendidly served. He sent, too, to those who asked for them, liquors, etc., as they could desire. Cooling drinks and fruits of all kinds were abundantly served every afternoon, and there were a number of little one and two horse vehicles always ready for the ladies and old men who liked a drive, besides play-tables in the apartments until supper time. A large number of the members of the Parliament did not go to Pontoise at all, but took advantage of the occasion to recreate themselves in the country. Only a few of the younger members mounted guard in the assembly, where nothing but the most trivial and make-believe business was conducted. Everything important was deliberately neglected. The Parliament, in a word, did nothing but divert itself, leave all business untouched, and laugh at the Regent and the government." The Parliament adhered to their resolution to refuse to register the edict, and remained in exile till the 17th of December.

Thus the final grand expedient of Law to restore the Company's fortunes was destroyed.

On the 17th of July an edict was published which prohibited the people from assembling in crowds, under pain of heavy penalties, and it was also declared to be necessary in the interests of public peace and safety to close the Bank for an indefinite period, and that no further notes could be received there for conversion into coin.

CHAPTER XII

Starvation produced amongst poorer classes by issue of new edict—Law's expulsion from France demanded—Law resigns all his offices and leaves for Venice—Privileges of Company withdrawn—Commission appointed to value unliquidated securities—Law in vain applies for recovery of a portion of his wealth—His death at Venice—Attitude of French people towards Law—Circumstances to be considered in passing judgment.

CHAPTER XII

The creation of twenty-five millions of perpetual annuities at two and one-half percent, and four millions of life annuities at four percent, in June as a means of absorbing notes to that extent was not attended with the success which had been anticipated. While the interest was small, it yet offered greater security than the notes themselves afforded, and on that ground alone ought to have appealed to holders of large amounts who were debarred by edicts from employing their paper in other directions for investment. Only a few possessed sufficient confidence to take advantage of the annuities, and the issue was accordingly of very insignificant amount. Law, however, was determined to secure the issue of the whole amount, and if necessary to do so by artificial means. His determination was made the stronger by the refusal of Parliament to agree to his last proposal. Accordingly, on the 15th of August, an edict was published which declared that all notes of 1000 livres in value and upwards should have no currency and would be regarded as cancelled, except those which were utilised either for purchase of annuities, or for opening credit accounts at the Bank, or for the payment of the uncalled liability on the new shares issued by the Company. This was followed by a second edict on the 10th of October, containing provisions of a similar nature with reference to all other notes, and requiring their utilisation before the 1st of November.

These drastic regulations had the effect of withdrawing from circulation a large quantity of paper, but still there were many holders who refused to part with their notes although rapidly becoming valueless. Some refused in the belief that their wealth might probably in the future become more liquid at its nominal value; others because their paper was required for ordinary daily purposes and could not therefore be spared for permanent investment. As a result, the country found itself on the 1st of November in possession of notes of enormous aggregate value which had automatically become absolutely worthless. Since the issue of the edicts, the trading community refused to accept payment in notes of goods supplied except at ruinous rates of discount, amounting in instances to eighty and ninety percent. Provisions and all classes of necessaries reached extravagant prices, and being unattainable by the poorer people, starvation reigned in the homes of thousands not only in Paris itself but also in the provinces. Decrees were issued fixing the maximum prices of food, but these were openly disregarded by every merchant, who could not have sold at the prices named without incurring loss to themselves. The difficulty in securing food and other necessaries had also been increased by the operations of wealthy speculators, who during the previous months of the year had purchased all available supplies with the paper in their possession and stored them in secret places or transported them from the country for realisation and for investment of the proceeds in foreign securities. Complaints, accordingly, continually reached the Government from those who were unable to satisfy the demands of the traders, and the Government was compelled to visit the culprits with the penalties they had power to impose, which included not only physical punishment but confiscation of all their goods, and frequently the payment of a heavy fine. The bakers of Paris suffered most from the tyrannical edicts, and, on one occasion, no fewer than eighteen were fined, placed in the stocks, and had their goods confiscated.

The final edict, published during the period of Law's management of the Bank and of the Company, appeared on the 24th of October, which directed that all the original shareholders of the Company who still retained their shares should deposit these with the Company, and that those who had sold the whole or part of their shares should now purchase the necessary number from the Company to make up the total of their original holdings at the price of 13,500 livres per share. To provide for the new purchases which this edict required an additional 50,000 shares were created, so that on the assumption that this number represented the minimum necessary to make up the deficiencies of holdings the Company would have absorbed over 600,000,000 livres of depreciated paper. But the edict contained the elements of its own destruction. It was impossible of accomplishment. The victims refused to purchase from the Company shares for 13,500 livres which were obtainable in the market for a mere tithe of that sum, and many of them immediately prepared to leave the country with all their belongings. So general were these preparations that no person was allowed to cross the frontier without the permission of the Regent on pain of death. The closest watch was kept upon all the main highways, and numerous arrests were made of suspected emigrants. Many millions of livres and considerable quantities of plate and jewellery, which their possessors attempted to smuggle across the frontiers, were seized and appropriated, the culprits being sent back to Paris to undergo punishment. In no case however was the extreme penalty imposed, confiscation and ruin being mercifully judged sufficient punishment.

Law's position was now becoming highly critical. On the

one hand the people were clamouring for his expulsion from the country, and even for his life. On the other hand, the Parliament, still at Pontoise, had not forgotten the author of their exile. His ingenuity had been used to the utmost to escape from the daily accumulating complications which surrounded him. All his efforts had failed in their purpose, and now he was resourceless. He stood alone a foreigner in a hostile country. His erstwhile friends had now deserted him, the tie of friendship broken by his inability to further increase their fortunes. One man, and one alone, the Regent himself, remained faithful to the last, and yet not openly. The safety of the crown forbade the Regent from employing his influence and power in order to retain the financier in his service, and prohibited him from ignoring indefinitely the demands of the people.

Law, accordingly, perceiving the extreme folly and danger of further continuing to direct the affairs of the Bank and of the Company, resolved after consultation with the Regent to resign the offices he still retained. He was anxious to leave the country at the same time, but the Regent considered such a step impolitic and refused to grant permission. He was allowed, however, to leave Paris, and retire to his estate at Guermande, which he did on the 13th of December. At the interview he had with the Regent before his departure, he advised the appointment of Pelletier de la Houssaye as Comptroller-General of Finances, and in referring to the failure of his schemes is said to have remarked, "I confess I have committed many faults. I committed them because I am a man, and all men are liable to error; but I declare to you most solemnly that none of them proceeded from wicked or dishonest motives, and that nothing of that kind will be found in the whole course of my conduct." Two days after his departure, Law received from the Regent a letter according permission to depart from the kingdom, and informing him that the Duke of Bourbon had been ordered to send him the necessary passports and such money as he might require for his journey. Two messengers arrived at Guermande on the following day, bringing the passports and a large sum of money, but Law respectfully refused to accept the latter. The postchaise of Madame de Prié, with an escort of six horse guards was also sent for his conveyance, and in it he set out with his son for Brussels on the 16th of December. On his way Law was unfortunately recognised by the Governor of Valenciennes and arrested as an ordinary fugitive from the kingdom. This was due to Law having offered passports drawn in another name, his identity being known to the Governor. He thereupon produced a second passport in his own name, but this only served to increase the perplexity of the Governor, who replied that the authorities frequently granted to men such as he, passports of convenience, because they had not the courage to refuse and that therefore he was still bound to prevent his departure. Law then produced a letter from the Regent to the Duke of Bourbon, in which the passports had been forwarded, and having thus satisfied the Governor of their genuineness he was allowed to proceed. On arrival at Brussels, on the 22nd of December, he was welcomed by the Marquis de Prié, Governor of the Imperial Low Countries, and enjoyed his hospitality while he rested before resuming his journey to Venice. Of all his vast wealth he took with him into exile the small sum of 36,000 livres, and two diamond rings of great value, one of which he sent to Madame de Prié on returning her carriage to her from Brussels. Law's wife and daughter remained in Paris for a short time after his departure, but joined him later in Venice after having realised sufficient to discharge all household debts due by them.

The rumour of Law's flight soon spread throughout Paris, and the Duke of Bourbon was saddled by the community with the responsibility of allowing his escape. The Regent, who had

instructed permission to be given, had by acting through the
Duke relieved himself, so far as the public were concerned,
of any blame in the matter. He had displayed considerable
astuteness in thus shifting the responsibility, but he had not
been altogether disinterested in the safety of the fugitive, and
had not acted from motives of friendship alone. The meeting of
the Regency Council held, on the 26th of January, to consider
the financial situation, disclosed a set of circumstances of a
highly incriminating character against the Regent, and revealed
the extreme advisability on his part of securing the departure of
Law before the return of Parliament to Paris, lest that assembly
should cause him to be arrested. The new Comptroller-General
had since his appointment on the 12th of December been
occupied in the attempt to unravel the complicated finances
of the kingdom, and had prepared a report for submission to
the Council. This was in fact the first occasion upon which the
members had been fully acquainted with the actual position,
their complete subservience to the Regent having hitherto
caused them to acquiesce in all the proposals presented to them
for approval.

La Houssaye reported that since the 22nd of May,
600,000,000 livres of banknotes had been issued by Law for
which there had been no authorisation by the Council, or by
the proprietors of the Bank. The question was discussed as
to whether the State or the Bank were in the circumstances
debtors to the holders, since the liability should be determined
according as they agreed that Law had issued them as
Comptroller-General or as manager of the Bank. The Duke of
Bourbon took the side of the Bank and was supported in his
contention by the Prince of Conti. La Houssaye, however, was
firm in his opinion that the excess of notes should be met by the
Bank, although it appeared that decrees had been issued by the
Regent of which the Council were ignorant. The Regent, pressed

by the Duke to give an explanation of his proceedings, stated that Law had created the notes on his own authority alone and that in order to save him from the possible consequences of his action, he had validated the notes by antedated decrees. "Then," replied the Duke, "Law in reality created these notes by your orders; otherwise you would not have allowed him to leave the kingdom and escape the consequences of a capital crime." The Regent retorted, "It was you who handed him the passports." "It is true," said the Duke, "but it was you who sent them to me. I never asked for them; you wished that he should leave the kingdom; and I can very easily explain the circumstances to the King and to the Council. I never advised that Law should depart, but I was opposed to his being handed over to the Parliament, because I believed that it was not to your interest to sanction this after having made use of him as you had; but I never asked you to let him leave the realm, and I beg you in presence of the King and before all these gentlemen to say if I ever did." "At least," said the Regent, "I did not order you to lend him your carriage, nor a guard to escort him; you interested yourself more in him than it was my intention. I allowed him to leave because his presence might have injured public credit and prejudice our recovery from the misfortunes into which we have fallen." It was clear to all those who were present that both the Duke and the Regent were equally afraid to have left Law to the mercy of the Parliament, as he might have proved them authors and accomplices of all that he had done. In their own interests, they had both played their parts badly at the Council table, but all recognised that the Duke only played a very minor part in the affair, and that the Regent throughout had been the real culprit, having compelled Law to issue the notes in order that he might satisfy his own extravagant

Notwithstanding the efforts of the Duke of Bourbon and of the Prince of Conti to make the government responsible for the excess of notes, and thus relieve the shareholders by increasing the free assets upon which they could claim in liquidation, La Houssaye gained his point, and reported that the public debt including the shares of the Company amounted to over thirty-one hundred million livres and bore interest to the extent of almost a hundred million livres per annum. So great a charge upon the revenues of the State could not be faced by the Government, but he recognised it was necessary to minimise as far as possible the loss which would require to be borne by the shareholders and possessors of banknotes, who, it was estimated numbered no less than 100,000 families. He accordingly proposed to withdraw all the privileges of the Company as far as these related to the management of the national revenues, and reduce it to the position of a mere trading concern. He would submit to the closest scrutiny the history of every individual holding either shares or notes and those which were tainted with speculation would be subject to cancellation. A commission would be appointed under whose supervision the work of investigation would be carried on, and all those who failed to submit their securities for adjudication before the 1st of August would be deprived entirely of any right to have a value placed upon their securities.

A decree to this effect was issued on the 4th of February, and immediately thereafter the Commission set to work. The task of investigation which covered transactions over half a million in number, and of a value of over 3000,000,000 livres, was entrusted to the brothers Paris, who employed for the purpose a staff of 800 clerks. To simplify the gigantic task, securities were cast into five categories according as they were:

(i) Reimbursements made by the King;
(ii) Reimbursements between private individuals;
(iii) Sales of real property;

(iv) Sales of personal property; and

(v) Purely speculative transactions.

All securities embraced in the fifth class were cancelled without consideration. The first were untouched because of their origin. The other three classes were subjected to reduction, ranging from five to ninety-five percent. By the end of 1721, the Commission were in a position to deliver their decision upon the first batch of securities, and by the end of the following year to finally bring their work to a conclusion. As a result of the investigation, 1000 million livres of securities were altogether cancelled, leaving a public debt of 2000 million livres bearing annual interest amounting to 48 million livres. The capital of the Company which had before the commission amounted to 200,000 shares was reduced to 56,000 shares of the value of 500 livres each, bearing a fixed dividend of 100 livres for the first year, and 150 livres during subsequent years, guaranteed by the Government and subject to increase, should the profits of the Company warrant it.

In the fifth category of securities, the brothers Paris caused the whole of the properties belonging to Law and to his brother William to be classed, an act of revenge for the failure of the *anti-system* with which they had identified themselves three years before. Law made several efforts to recover at least a portion of his wealth, but they were of no avail, and the subsequent years of his life were years of misery and often times direst poverty. After wandering about the Continent for several months, he returned to England in October, 1721, and resided in London until 1725, in which year he returned to Venice, whither he had proceeded on his departure from France. Here he remained until his death on the 21st of March, 1729, leading the precarious life of a gambler and general speculator and leaving at his death the valuable ring which alone had escaped the arbitrary and cruel proceedings of his enemies in France.

For several generations after the downfall of the System, Law was held in deep and bitter hatred by the people of France. The name of the author of the System was associated, not unnaturally, with the financial ruin which it brought to so many individuals, and it was convenient that those who were really responsible for its disastrous end should foster that attitude of hostility to the man who was now unable to appeal to the better reason of the people. It is perfectly clear that at no time did Law seek to advance alone his own material interests by the schemes he put into operation. No circumstance reveals this more clearly than the fact that at the date of his flight all his possessions were in France and that no attempt was made by him during the latter half of 1720 to transfer any part of his wealth to foreign countries for safety, although events were at that period rapidly leading to a financial collapse and determining many to pursue such a course as a measure of prudent provision for the future. Law himself puts this very forcibly in a letter written on the 15th of October, 1724, to the Duke of Bourbon, in which he seeks that nobleman's interest on his behalf in his efforts to secure the restitution of at least a portion of the wealth he left behind him. "The Company owes its birth to me. For them I have sacrificed everything, even my property and my credit, being now bankrupt, not only in France, but also in all other countries. For them I have sacrificed the interest of my children, whom I tenderly love, and who are deserving of all my affection; these children, courted by the most considerable families in France, are now destitute of fortune and of establishments. I had it in my power to have settled my daughter in marriage in the first houses of Italy, Germany, and England; but I refused all offers of that nature, thinking it inconsistent with my duty to, and my affection for, the state in whose service I had the honour to be engaged. I do not assume to myself any merit from this conduct, and I never so much as spoke upon the subject to the Regent. But I cannot help observing that this mode of behaviour is diametrically opposite to the idea my enemies wish to impute to me; and surely all Europe ought to have a good opinion of my disinterestedness, and of the condition to which I am reduced, since I no longer receive any proposals of marriage for my children.

My Lord, I conducted myself with a still greater degree of delicacy, for I took care not to have my son or my daughter married even in France, although I had the most splendid and advantageous offers of that kind. I did not choose that any part of my protection should be owing to alliances, but that it should depend solely upon the intrinsic merits of my project."

In passing judgment upon Law, it is necessary to remember that the principles upon which he proceeded while he had himself absolute control of the management of his System were economically sound. Elements of unsoundness only appeared from the time when the management passed under the supervision of the Regent. He it was who insisted upon the adoption of measures which to Law appeared fraught with the gravest consequences and which he was unable to resist. Had Law been able to work out his own designs, unhampered by the dictation of the Regent, it is conceivable that he might in time have realised his ambition of placing the finances of his adopted country upon a just and stable foundation. Even as it was he succeeded to an extent surprising in the circumstances. Financial corruption was no longer possible to the great extent to which it proceeded in the days of Louis XIV. Numerous offices in the patronage of the Government to which large emoluments and no duties were attached, and many privileges and monopolies which had hitherto checked the progress of industry, were abolished never to be revived. Agriculture improved, new industries arose, valuable public works were undertaken, and in general, a healthier industrial atmosphere was created throughout the country. That France did not take full advantage of the great principles of sound industrial progress which were formulated for them and advocated by Law was neither the fault of him nor of his System. It was the fault of the people themselves, who were yet to find that resort to violence was to prove the only means of removing the great obstacles which stood in the way of their advancement as a nation.

THE END

INDEX

MORE FROM NEWTON PAGE

The Life of John Law
John Philip Wood
ISBN-13: 9781934619018

**The Financier, Law: His Scheme and Times. A Graphic Description
of the Origin, Maturity and Wreck of the Mississippi Scheme**
André Cochut
ISBN-13: 9781934619049

**The Mississippi Bubble:
A Memoir of John Law**
Adolphe Thiers
ISBN-13: 9781934619056

**John Law's Money and Trade Considered:
A Hidden Foundation of Modern Economic Thought**
Gavin John Adams
ISBN-13: 9781934619094

Letters to John Law
Gavin John Adams
ISBN-13: 9781934619087

Newton Page books are available at all good bookstores and online
book retailers. For more information about our books and how to order
them, please visit our website:

www.newtonpage.com

Made in the USA
San Bernardino, CA
10 August 2017